THE LENNON PROPHECY

Joseph Niezgoda

THE LENNON PROPHECY

A NEW EXAMINATION OF THE DEATH CLUES OF THE BEATLES

New Chapter Press

The Lennon Prophecy is published by New Chapter Press (www.newchapterpressmedia.com) and is distributed by the Independent Publishers Group (www.ipgbook.com).

ISBN-978-0942257458

For more information on this story—and for further clues— go to
www.TheLennonProphecy.com

Contents

"What have I done to deserve such a fate?
I realize I have left it too late.
And so it's true, pride comes before a fall.
I'm telling you so that you won't lose all."

— John Lennon, "I'm a Loser," 1964

Do You Want To Know A Secret?

I've sold my soul to the devil.
— John Lennon

The Beatles first landed in the United States on February 7, 1964. It was a Friday. It was also my eighth birthday.

On the school-bus ride home, some older girls were sitting ahead of me and one of them said, "Oh, The Beatles are on *Ed Sullivan* this weekend." I didn't know what that meant. I didn't know what The Beatles were. But I did know I was going to watch *Ed Sullivan*.

I remember sitting that Sunday night in front of the family television with my parents and my brother Mick. The show opened with the traditional shot of the empty lit set, and I remember the announcer bellowing, "And now, here he is … Ed Sullivan!" In my mind I can still see the iconic host walking from the wings to his spot on stage, dressed in a suit and diagonal-striped tie, a white handkerchief peeking from his breast pocket, his hair slicked back, nodding a head-bow to the cheering studio crowd. I remember him explaining the excitement that had been stirring around the production all week, how hundreds of news writers and photographers had descended upon his theater. And he wasted no time introducing his most special British guests; just a half minute into the show he called out, "Ladies and gentlemen … The Beatles!" And the young crowd, barely obeying the laws of gravity as they bounced in their seats, yelled and screamed in ways never before witnessed on national television, all in reverence for a band that had never previously performed on American soil. The camera cut to the boys from Liverpool standing center in a circle of large prop arrows, each pointing toward the focus of 73 million American television viewers. I remember Paul McCartney turning toward his mates, nodding a count, singing the words "close your eyes," and the band simultaneously starting in together on the music for the song "All My Loving."

I was instantly a fan.

Like so many others across the country and around the world, I became fascinated with the Fab Four. They were absolutely my idols. And John Lennon, in particular, I idolized the most. In fact, he's the only person I have ever felt that way about. I've been a lifelong music fan, and a lifelong sports fan, but no other individual has stirred such adulation in me. That admiration was shared by my brother and my mother, both of whom were also avid music fans. My mom still has a Mother's Day card from 1967 that's signed, "With love, your boys, Joe, Mick and John Lennon."

I had all The Beatles' albums. My cousins gave some to me as I was growing up, and in 1967 I bought my own for the first time, spending $3.18 of hard-earned snow-shoveling money on a copy of the brand-new *Magical Mystery Tour* record. Between my older sister Linda and me, we owned all The Beatles' singles. We listened to the songs so much that I came to memorize the lyrics sheerly from auditory repetition. We used to play a game wherein someone would recite three consecutive words from a Beatles composition, and I could name the song. I also avidly read about the band, and to this day I can recall all that information—it just stuck in my consciousness. When I began playing guitar, the first song I learned on my uncle's hollowbody Gibson electric was "Ballad of John and Yoko."

Years later, on the evening of December 8, 1980, I was in my dorm room at King's College in Pennsylvania, watching Monday Night Football with my study partner Mike. That's when my life changed. Commentator Howard Cosell announced that John had been shot and killed in New York City.

I was in absolute disbelief. I said to Mike, "They made a mistake. It can't be."

Later that evening, the reality of John's death set in. I still remember the feeling inside me. I couldn't sleep. I was sick. I had lived a charmed life to that point—aside from my grandmother, no one who had any real value or meaning to me had passed away. It really hurt deep. I made a black arm band to wear for a week. I also listened to the radio all night—every station seemed to be playing Beatles and Lennon songs. The next morning, I read about the assassination in every newspaper I could find.

Then something else happened—something that changed my life even more, though I didn't know it at the time. I'd been recording the night's radio tributes on cassette tapes, for no particular reason; I didn't know why I'd been doing it, and still don't. One of the tapes already contained some music: songs by Badfinger, a group that had recorded in The Beatles' Apple Studios, a group that had purportedly gotten its name from "Bad Finger Boogie," the original title of John's composition "With a Little Help From My Friends."[1] Tuesday morning I was playing back one of the radio broadcasts, and it ended with the disc jockey saying, "John Lennon, dead, at 40 years old." I pressed the stop button and pondered the reality for about the thousandth time. Then, just to humor an inexplicable curiosity, I flipped the tape over to hear what was recorded in the same spot on the other side. I pressed play, and it was perfectly cued to Badfinger's song "Sweet Tuesday Morning." That really freaked me out—not so much because it happened to be Tuesday morning in Pennsylvania, but because I realized that at the moment John had been shot, it had been Tuesday morning in his hometown of Liverpool, England. Moreover, I knew that Badfinger's Joey Molland wrote and recorded that song at the same time he was working with John Lennon on the *Imagine* album.

---

1   Matovina, p. 67

I listened closely to the lyrics:

> *Sweet Tuesday morning, came and you smiled,*
> *Love was the answer you gave me.*

I thought, "Yes, that's what John preached: Love is the answer." The song continued:

> *I've been to places all around, astound me.*
> *I've seen the breaking of the souvenir.*

I wondered, What could that possibly mean, "the breaking of the souvenir"? Then I soon learned that before being murdered, John had autographed an album for his shooter, Mark David Chapman.

That string of relationships between facts was, I thought, too uncanny to be coincidence. Over the next several years, more clues appeared. I rarely looked for them; they just seemed to arrive in front of me, uninvited but clear and concise. I often discussed them with Mick—we'd talk on the phone for hours, rehashing lyrics from songs and tidbits from articles and backgrounds in photographs. But I still didn't know what it all meant. Then one day the answer just came to me. And again, I felt sick about something related to The Beatles.

Could John Lennon have sold his soul to the devil?

I was angered because I thought it crazy that he would do something like this. I was upset and disappointed.

I was, of course, not the first person to notice possible hidden clues in Beatles history. Nor was I the first to wonder about the band's enigmatic success.

The Beatles—John Lennon, Paul McCartney, George Harrison and Ringo Starr—rose from utter obscurity in Liverpool, England, and in only a few years captured the attention and imagination of the world. It was the 1960s, a time when music was more than just a pastime for passionate fans; it was also a cultural phenomenon that created a storm of social change throughout the industrial world.

The Beatles were the eye of that storm. Their success transcended stardom and understanding. The image they portrayed—long hair, dress, attitude, humor and lifestyle—at once led and reflected the transformation of a generation. Unlike other rock 'n' roll bands, The Beatles had a perplexing effect on the masses. Wherever they traveled, the boys from Liverpool were met by thousands and thousands of screaming, sobbing and hysterical fans, even at unscheduled stops. Old newspaper clippings, news films, books and magazine articles don't begin to reflect even half of what the craze was like; no journalistic portrayal has been able to fully convey the cultural delirium. The Beatles achieved near god-like worship from fans around the world. Girls went to their concerts and wept uncontrollably; they covered their ears and screamed at the mere sight of the band. Boys as well were lured by their charm. Audiences were described as hypnotic, spellbound, transfixed and in ecstasy. Nothing before or after came close to equaling the rapid, widespread emotional sensation surrounding these four young men from England. The public's overwhelming response was so unique that it was given its own name: "Beatlemania." And while other entertainers have since matched or bettered Beatles' record sales, no one has managed to equal their universal popularity.

Moreover, all that hysteria and mania left the world dumbfounded.

From the very beginning of The Beatles' success, people asked: Why the mayhem? What did these four men have that no one else did? What could possibly explain the rapid and spontaneous worldwide overreaction to this band? Their songs were no more catchy and lyrical than those of The Kinks or The Rolling Stones, and they were never highly regarded as live performers. Many have speculated that the cult following was produced not just by the music, but also by The Beatles' personalities. They seemed to possess a kind of magic. Where that magic came from was always a mystery.

Of course, mysteries unsolved grow more fascinating as time passes. Something beckons us to reexamine them. We relentlessly pore over the evidence; we analyze every angle and clue. And sometimes what we can uncover can be truly unbelievable and frightening. One clue about the mystery of The

Beatles' success may come from a simple statement John Lennon made in the middle of the 1960s, at a time when the world idolized him, when nearly every creative decision he made changed the course of culture, when he was traveling the globe meeting presidents, kings and queens, and when he was selling millions of records and performing for millions of spectators and being mobbed by millions of fans. At the height of that very popularity, John said to his friend Tony Sheridan: "I've sold my soul to the devil."[2]

Mystery also surrounds the star's untimely death. On December 8, 1980—almost 20 years to the day that The Beatles became a sudden sensation—John Lennon was gunned down in the archway leading to the Dakota Apartments in New York City. Was his murder really a random, senseless act committed by a deranged fan, or is there a greater story to tell?

As a teenager, John had a strong desire to be rich and world-famous. In the very early days of The Beatles, he would say, "Where we going, fellas?" and the others would respond, "To the toppermost of the poppermost!"[3] In his desperation for stardom, could John really have turned to the devil to fulfill his dreams? Did John go so far as to enter into a contract with Satan in exchange for 20 years of wealth, women and fame? Were the circumstances that led to John's violent death the result of this pact?

Furthermore, how could these questions even be answerable? One needs only to look in a place millions already have: the music.

The idea that Beatles compositions contain hidden messages is almost as old as the band itself. During the late 1960s, the public began noticing cryptic communications on Beatles album covers, in pictures and in the lyrics, all of which seemed to reveal or foretell the death of someone in the band. Once analyzed, the collective belief was that the doomed member was Paul McCartney, and the body of evidence became known as the "Paul-is-Dead Clues." The analysis supposedly revealed that at 5 a.m. on November 9, 1966, Paul was killed in an automobile accident and was replaced in the band by a look- and sound-alike musician. Supporting clues included lyrics such as "He blew his mind out in a car" from the song "A Day in the Life," and "Wednesday morning at 5 o'clock" from "She's Leaving Home." The Beatles—Paul, in

---

2   Coleman, p. 348
3   *The Beatles Anthology*, p. 68

particular—denied the rumors. But that never quenched the public's desire to continue dissecting the group's material. For one thing, the messages weren't going away; on the contrary, they were becoming more frequent. Something strange was going on. Everyone, on some level, knew it.

Not only were the messages hinting of death, but some were being delivered in ways associated with the occult. Many people believe that the devil's presence and power is exposed in backward communication, in mirror images, and in words and symbols that have double meanings. All of these can be found in The Beatles' work. In fact, the first cases of reversed sounds in rock 'n' roll history were produced by The Beatles. John Lennon pioneered the technique. In his song "Rain," he included five backward segments of music and words; in "Tomorrow Never Knows," music was sped up and slowed down and reversed; and the same technique was used again in "Strawberry Fields Forever." Those were all deliberate manipulations, but other voice reversals in Beatles songs are even more eerie, because they are seemingly unintentional. Two of the most clear instances are in the songs "Revolution 9" and "I'm So Tired." Both tracks, played backward, distinctly mention a "dead man."

There is no doubt John was aware of these messages—by the late 1960s, most of the civilized world was aware. But did he first learn about the clues from the public or through his own observation? And if the clues weren't singling out Paul, then who? Did John recognize the clues as being about his *own* death, about his spiritual transgression, about his bargain for unfathomable fame?

I believe the answer is yes, and this book is my proof.

No one is sorrier than I about what is written here. It's a horrifying topic and a difficult subject for me. I wish my interpretation was wrong.

Nonetheless, I remain a fan. My wife has asked me, "How can you still listen to those songs the same way, knowing what you know?" I have no answer. I never did understand why I was obsessed, even when I was eight years old watching *Ed Sullivan*. Like millions upon millions of fans from nearly every arc of the globe, I just absolutely can't hear enough of that music.

John was a phenomenal song writer and performer. I still feel such sorrow for him. I enjoyed his music. I enjoyed the way he looked. I enjoyed his performing skills, and his voice. He is still very much alive in his music, and very much alive in my heart.

I still mourn John Lennon. But I have to accept what I believe he did.

—Joseph Niezgoda, 2008

A Pact With The Devil

Once the circle has been drawn and the devil conjured,
there is no avoiding the pact; and unfortunates who desire
to bargain with the devil over the terms, found to their sorrow that
there was but one form that Lucifer would agree to, and that
was that he agreed to help the magician in every way,
and provide him with all the gold and jewels that he desired,
providing that the sorcerer gave himself over to Satan body and
soul after 20 years, for any purpose that the devil wished.
The devil, after having received the pact, written or
signed in blood, took it to hell with him, and kept it as security.
— Ebenezer Sibley, *A Key to Physic, and the Occult Sciences*

Some people expect immediate payment in life. And when the toil and struggle to maintain their soul in a heavenly bond goes beyond their strength and endurance, some summon the devil. They follow him blindly and are enticed and taken captive.

Or so the stories go.

Whether the sway of Satan is real or imagined, a spiritual truth or a psychological effect, is, of course, uncertain to most of us. Without proof, the existence of that power, the existence of the devil himself, remains a matter of faith. But regardless of whether one trusts that power as true, the fact remains that many of the world's major religions recognize the devil or a comparable concept, some kind of prince or supreme being of evil, or a similar warden of temptation or deception. Throughout history an untold number of people—certainly millions—have believed very much in the power of Satan. And some of those have staked their afterlife on his word.

Stories of people making deals with the devil are as old as humankind. According to the Bible's book of Genesis, even the first humans God created forfeited to Satan's power. In the story of the temptation of Eve in the Garden of Eden, God asks, "What is it that you have done?" Eve replies, "The serpent tricked me and I ate."

Since that first alliance with the underworld, many riddles have weighed upon the human heart—anguish, dilemma and an infinite list of predicaments. In response, some humans bargained with the devil for solutions, including prominent position, power, protection, love interests, sexual pleasure, wealth and learning. Through these pacts, people aimed to obtain things ranging from simple desires to the extraordinary. The end of their bargain, though, was not as beneficial as the beginning: The devil traditionally collected his souls by means of a terrifying and violent death.

The protagonists of these tales are not solely among the obscure names of history. The lives of many notable people show evidence—either circumstantial or biographical—that they, too, have pursued dealings with the devil. Among these are Socrates, Nostradamus, Galileo and Martin Luther.[1] The most famous modern example is that of 1930s blues musician Robert Johnson, who allegedly traded his soul for the ability to expertly play guitar, then tried to renege on the deal, both of which he wrote songs about.

Even popes have not been free from the accusation of dealing with Satan. Alexander VI was suspected of such consorts in the late 1400s. His character

---

1   Rudwin, p. 187

was so dubious that when he was elected pope, another religious icon of the time, Giovanni di Lorenzo de' Medici (who would later become Pope Leo X), remarked, "Now we are in the power of a wolf, the most rapacious perhaps that this world has ever seen. And if we do not flee, he will inevitably devour us all."[2] And the 10th-century story of Pope Sylvester II is an infamous tale of a man who sold his soul to the devil—in exchange for the papacy.[3] The list continues: Popes Caelestinus, Gregory VII, Paul II and Alexander VI were all thought to have conspired with the underworld.[4]

Sylvester's story includes another common theme in deals with the devil: The exact means and timing of the victim's final payment have not always been transparent. This appears to be a fail-safe for Satan, a way to close loopholes that his contractees may try to escape through. People who enter into these pacts are generally aware of their allotted time, and, not surprisingly, they may try to avoid confronting Satan as the end draws near. So Satan tricks them. According to *Liber Pontificalis* (the "Book of the Popes"): "[Sylvester] asked how long he would live as pope. The

Pope Sylvester II, whose papacy began in 999, is one figure in history thought to have sold his soul to the devil.

answer was, as long as he wanted to, unless he said mass at Jerusalem. He rejoiced, thinking he was far away from death, as far as he was from the

2   Reston, p. 287
3   Ambrosini, p. 91
4   Rudwin, p. 188

desire to go on a pilgrimage to Jerusalem. But during Lent he said mass at the Lateran in a church called Jerusalem.

"He heard the rattling of the demon and at the same time felt death was approaching. And sighing, he started to cry."[5]

Arturo Graf, author of *The Story of the Devil*, offers a further example of Satan's cunning in collection: "It is related of a poor youth of Loreto ... [who] became enamored of a certain woman and had sinful commerce with her. Falling ill without warning, and his end being at hand, in a contrite spirit he regrets his error and makes a most devout confession, so that those present are fully assured of his salvation. But at the last moment, when he was about to expire, lo, the devil appeared to him in the guise of the woman that he loved, and asked him, in a voice broken with sobs: 'Wilt thou forsake me, then, my love?' At that sight and at those words, the poor fellow, forgetting himself and seized with a last spasm of affection, rallies what little breath is left and murmurs, 'Never will I forsake thee, my beloved!' Immediately he dies, and the devil carries his soul off to hell for all eternity."

Another interesting aspect of the pope conspiracies is that the devil's contract requires that the signer commit blasphemy, allegedly because that sacrilegious act is what allows Satan to collect his debt. Maximilian Rudwin, author of *The Devil in Legend and Literature*, writes: "The devil, notwithstanding the great power he possesses over the bodies and minds of mortals, is, however, not potent enough to put a man to death, unless his victim has blasphemed or renounced the lord." Rudwin also notes that Satan is specific in his demand for "a formal denial of the Christian faith, a rejection of Christian symbols and a renunciation of the lord and his saints. ... [The victim is also] forced to express a hatred for all Christians and a promise to resist all attempts to convert him."

Furthermore, an agreement with hell mandates reciprocal obligations in the form of recognizing the devil's power. Not only does the signer have to renounce God, but he or she must also revere Satan. In the Bible, the devil

---

Dr. Johann Faust's life exhibited the perfect model of a deal with the devil. His story, perhaps the most well-known of a person to have entered into a pact with Satan, was confirmed by many contemporaries including a Protestant minister.

requests this even from Jesus: Satan shows the son of God the kingdoms of the earth and says, "All this I will give you, if you fall down and worship me."[6]

All of this inspires the question: What is typical of a supposed sale of one's soul to Satan? The perfect model of a pact can be seen in a solitary story, that of Dr. Johann Faust. The protagonist of countless pieces of drama and fiction, Faust was indeed a real person whose story was confirmed by many contemporaries who knew him or knew of him, including a Protestant minister. Faust's tale first appeared in print around 1587, nearly half a century after his death, in *Historia von D. Johann Fausten*, published by Johann Spies. More popular versions appeared later as *The Tragical History of Doctor Faustus* by Christopher Marlowe in 1604, and *Faust—The Tragedy* by Johann Wolfgang von Goethe in 1808 (Part 1) and 1832 (Part 2). All tell the story of Faust as a young and devoted student with a voracious appetite for learning, not uncommon for Renaissance men. Faust yearned to know all things, to do all things and to enjoy all things. But he felt ungratified. He believed that his formal education was not quenching his thirst for knowledge, nor was it settling his restless desire for

pleasure. So he instead turned to dealing with magic. He conjured the demon
Mephistopheles and entered into a pact with the devil. The text of Faust's pact,
according to Spies:

"I, Johann Faustus, Dr.,

"Do publicly declare with mine own hand in covenant and by
power of these presents:

"Whereas, mine own spiritual faculties having been exhaustively
explored (including the gifts dispensed from above and gracious-
ly imparted to me), I still cannot comprehend;

"And whereas, it being my wish to probe further into the matter,
I do propose to speculate upon the Elementa;

"And whereas mankind doth not teach such things;

"Now therefore have I summoned the spirit who calleth himself Mephistopheles, a servant of the Hellish Prince in Orient,
charged with informing and instructing me, and agreeing against
a promissory instrument hereby transferred unto him to be sub-
servient and obedient to me in all things.

"I do promise him in return that, when I be fully sated of that
which I desire of him, twenty-four years also being past, ended
and expired, he may at such a time and in whatever manner or
wise pleaseth him order, ordain, reign, rule and possess all that
may be mine: body, property, flesh, blood, etc., herewith duly
bound over in eternity and surrendered by covenant in mine
own hand by authority and power of these presents, as well as of
my mind, brain, intent, blood and will.

"I do now defy all living beings, all the Heavenly Host and all mankind, and this must be.

"In confirmation and contract whereof I have drawn out mine own blood for certification in lieu of a seal."

The devil would provide to Faust all his desired exploits and knowledge for the agreed time period. In return, Faust would give his soul to Satan.

Apparently the deal worked. Faust, aided by Mephistopheles, became a well-known "necromancer, astrologer, alchemist, soothsayer and clairvoyant,"[7] traveling the countryside practicing his skills, journeying over all the earth and even through the heavens. He procured the most beautiful of women, acquired tremendous wealth and performed numerous miracles. He even boasted of performing more miracles than Jesus Christ.[8] People having the honor to meet Faust were charmed by his exploits. One such instance was when he traveled to the city of Erfurt, Germany, and gave a public reading from Homer's *Iliad*, clad in the armor of the ancient times, expressing himself in their language and attitudes. He offered to give Erfurt's university all the lost comedies of Roman playwrights Plautus and Terence, which he would recite to them in precise detail—from memory. But the university rejected his offer for fear they would be entering into a diabolic trap.

Faust richly enjoyed the benefits secured to him by his contract. However, in mortgaging his soul to Satan, he became irrevocably damned, lost and fallen to the power of evil. Centuries of stories demonstrate that dealing with the devil is a double-edged sword, for Satan always keeps his word. He will provide the pact signer all his or her desires; but those who make such contracts seem to live joyless and frantic lives, their psyches always shadowed by the horror awaiting at the end. Such was the case for Faust. In his later years, he began to show symptoms of repentance and remorse, and became depressed about his pending fate. As consolation, the devil delivered him a woman, the once-deceased Helen of Troy, as a distraction for his remaining years.

---

7   Cavendish, p. 845
8   Cavendish, p. 845

When Faust's final, fatal day arrived, he invited his friends to a banquet in the village of Rimlich, near the town of Wittenberg, and confided in them his story. He begged not to be left alone. They stayed, but to no avail. Shortly after midnight a strong gust of wind roared through the house, shaking the walls and foundation. The gathered friends heard horrible whispers of the devil, followed by Faust's desperate screams. They were stricken with fear—none dared to intervene. In the morning, they entered his bedroom to find blood everywhere, his eyes stuck to the walls, several of his teeth scattered on the floor and pieces of his brain strewn about the room. As for Faust's body, they later found it outdoors, mutilated and flung on a pile of dung.

Such is the way of a pact with Satan.

John Lennon: Of His Parentage And Birth

There are places I remember
All my life, though some have changed.
— John Lennon

The omen in Liverpool, England, on October 9, 1940, was inauspicious. An unprecedented violence threatened the very existence of the small seaport town, causing grief and worry amongst its inhabitants. Evil, in the guise of Germany's dictator Adolf Hitler, was falling all over England in the form of nightly bombing raids by Nazi warplanes. But life sprung amidst this turmoil; born to Freddie and Julia Lennon was a baby boy. John Winston Lennon arrived to a world mired in conflict, death and destruction in the early years of World War II.

Julia was unarmed to face the challenge and responsibility of motherhood. She possessed a lively personality with a frolicsome disposition that left her little time to nurture and raise an infant son. Early on, she tried to rear John alone, but when boyhood displaced infancy, her lifestyle of frequenting local pubs and bringing home uniformed men left John with feelings of anger and insecurity.[1] Freddie likewise lacked the sensibility to raise a child. As a sea steward, he was mostly absent from John's life, and his constant traveling caused dissension in his relationship with his family. It was in Freddie's absence that Julia began socializing at pubs and staying out into the early hours of morning. Once after returning home from nearly 18 months at sea, he found his wife pregnant with another man's baby.[2]

Perhaps inevitably, John became a pawn in his parents' broken relationship. Ray Coleman, John's official biographer, relays one such story in his book *Lennon: The Definitive Biography*. In 1946, Freddie arrived in Liverpool to find John rooming with his aunt, Mimi Smith, in the nearby village of Woolton. Freddie took John to stay with him in the seaside resort town of Blackpool, a place known for its sandy beaches and fun-filled distractions with plenty to attract the wonder of a 5-year-old boy. Freddie was planning to move to New Zealand and wanted to take John with him, but then Julia arrived to reclaim her son and return to Liverpool. An ugly scene unfolded between the parents. John watched and listened to them argue. Finally, Freddie turned to his son and said, "You have to decide if you want to stay with me or with Mummy." Having just spoiled John for several weeks in Blackpool, Freddie knew what the answer would be. John chose Daddy.

Julia said, "Now John, are you sure about that?" and John replied again, "With Daddy." But as Julia turned and walked out the door, John was immediately struck with her loss and ran out after her.

John never forgot the horror of that incident. It left a permanent scar and great feelings of insecurity, and nearly 20 years would pass before he would see his father again.

Though John chose to live with his mother, she was too preoccupied with her own life to adequately provide for his needs. On the evenings she stayed out late, John was left alone and he found sleeping difficult. One night he awoke to see a ghost standing outside his bedroom door, and began to scream

---

1   Seaman, p. 64
2   Goldman, p. 31

so frantically that neighbors ran to his house. Other nights his mother staggered home late with different men she'd met in the local pubs; later he recalled
that she had been "not prostituting for money but rather for silk stockings."

Yearning for a stable, comfortable and secure environment, he began running away from Julia, always with the same destination. At 6 years old, he
would board a train by himself, at first unsure of the direction, and travel several miles to be with Aunt Mimi in Woolton. "I learned to recognize the right
trolley by the quality of the black leather seat," John said when he was older.
"To this day I'm fond of black leather. I find it comforting." On these jaunts,
sometimes strangers would approach him, thinking he was a lost or abandoned
child, and take him to the local police station. "I could never find the right
words to explain my situation," he said.[3] As his visits became more and more
frequent, eventually Mimi took him in to live at 251 Menlove Avenue.

The circumstances of John's childhood hindered his attempts at happiness
at every stage of his young life, adding distress, malice and brashness to his
character—all of which began to pave the way of a dark path. He became a
child filled with internal rage and aggressiveness. At Dovedale Primary School
in Liverpool, he frequently clashed with teachers and classmates. Coleman
writes that the headmaster described John's character as "sharp as a needle,"
and that classmate and friend Doug Freeman admitted, "We were all a little
bit frightened of him … and it stuck out to parents that he was different. The
mothers had their eyes on him as if to say, 'Keep away from that one.'"

By the age of 9, John was clearly different from the other children. Aunt Mimi
and his uncle, George Smith, provided him with a stable and comfortable living environment, and with their adequate discipline John became a bold, quick
and ingenious boy. But as he grew older, the pain of a broken home continually surfaced. A sensitive and intelligent child, he could be forgiven for learning to camouflage his emotions of love with an outward show of toughness.
Scholastic programs failed to inspire him, and his brash, outlandish behavior

---

3   Seaman, p. 180-181

made him unpopular with teachers. Not only did he dislike schoolwork, but he hated being forced to do it.

John didn't mind working on his own, however. He was an avid reader, and Aunt Mimi remembered him being particularly interested in books that dealt with magic.[4] He had already become open to encounters with higher beings. According to Coleman, one day Mimi said John walked into the kitchen and exclaimed, "I've just seen God." She asked him what God was doing, and he replied, "Oh, just sitting by the fire." Coleman also notes that John would spend hours alone in his bedroom, sitting in front of the mirror, staring at his own face so intently that he would fall into a trance and hallucinate.

As a boy, John Lennon placed his dreams and hopes in magic, in a wish or a spell that would offer him a better life.

Another childhood story reflects even more on that same side of John, on the part of him that looked beyond the natural world for solutions. David Ashton, a friend since they were young lads in Woolton, later wrote an essay titled "The Vanished World of a Woolton Childhood with John Lennon." He describes a hidden spring in a field that John and some other friends showed him. Ashton writes, "They told us that the spring, which was beside an ivy-clad oak tree, was a Holy well and that if you told it your wishes and turned round twice it would all come true." Even as a young child John was placing his dreams and hope in magic, in a wish or a spell that would offer him a better life.

Starting in 1952, John attended Quarry Bank High School in Liverpool. According to Coleman, Aunt Mimi noticed an alarming and negative change in his behavior, so severe that she feared he would become notorious. All the definitive biographies of John characterize his high-school life the same: From his first day at Quarry Bank, he was uncooperative, disrespectful and

---

4   Coleman, p. 113

rambunctious, showing little patience or respect toward teachers and class assignments. His grades dropped from the top of his class to the bottom. School evaluations reported, "Certainly on the road to failure … hopeless … wasting other pupils' time." The headmaster viewed John as raucous, making no positive contributions to school life, a student whose three main attributes included "skipping class, swearing and smoking."[5] The discontent between teacher and pupil was mutual; John viewed the instructors as boring, and attached little importance to his academic work. He was tough and cruel to his teachers, attacking them in bizarre drawings that often included offensive language. He was bored, he ridiculed those involved in sporting activities, he cheated on exams, and he blatantly lied about everything wrong he was caught doing. He harassed students who appeared weak, he stole from candy shops, and he pilfered cigarettes to sell to make money.[6]

John also appeared to grow discontented with God—and he showed it. He was thrown out of religious chorus for substituting obscene words into songs. He appeared morally defiant, spiritually hostile and at odds with Jesus Christ and the Christian faith. In the book *The Gospel According to the Beatles*, author Steve Turner writes: "John regularly poked fun at church dignitaries, parodied hymns, and drew blasphemous cartoons of Christ on the cross in a way that only the once-faithful can." And in a *Liverpool Echo* article in 2005, an old friend tells of John stealing from St. Paul's Roman Catholic bookshop in Liverpool: "He used to go in there and nick things. It was almost as if he wanted to get struck down by a thunderbolt. He could have gone into Wool-worths, but no. He had to go into this particular shop. One of the things I re-member him taking was a book on Pope Pius XII. The devilment was always there, and it could be quite frightening."

John's troubled childhood gave him little reason for hope, as more and more security began to vanish. At 14, Uncle George—John's defender from Aunt Mimi's stubbornly stern demeanor—died suddenly. Another father figure had left, and John clung to its memory. Years after his death, he still wore one of his uncle's jackets to school.[7] The loss of his uncle also

---

5   Coleman, p. 108
6   Davies, p. 11
7   Coleman, p. 184

affected his relationship with his aunt. While later he said he was grateful to Mimi for providing him with a home, a deep divide developed between them in George's absence. Mimi was hard and cold, and inflexible with her discipline. It was not a forgiving environment for someone who already begrudged authority. "She tried to keep John in line by shaming or humiliating him; but when he failed to respond to psychological tactics, she would occasionally resort to conventional beatings," writes Frederic Seaman, John's personal assistant, in the book *The Last Days of John Lennon*. "He later blamed Mimi for bullying and suffocating him with her insistence on discipline and routine."

Worse still, Mimi would stifle his one constructive outlet. In a 1971 interview with *Rolling Stone* magazine, John recounts Mimi throwing away his artwork, and his response of unpalatable resentment. "I used to say to my auntie, 'You throw my fuckin' poetry out, and you'll regret it when I'm famous,' and she threw the bastard stuff out." He said he never forgave Mimi for discouraging his creative pursuits in art, including music. Later she would ban Paul McCartney and George Harrison from coming to the house and would prohibit John from playing in a group. For a long time he had to hide the fact that he played guitar and sang in a band. She would tell him, "A guitar is all right for a hobby, John, but it won't earn you any money."

But after the emergence of Elvis Presley and his song "Heartbreak Hotel" in 1956, there would be no restraining John's ambition. He was completely captivated by rock 'n' roll music and Elvis became his idol. In Phillip Norman's book *Shout!*, Mimi recalls, "From then on, I never got a minute's peace. It was Elvis Presley, Elvis Presley, Elvis Presley. In the end I said, 'Elvis Presley's all very well, John, but I don't want him for breakfast, dinner, and tea.'"

In Elvis, John had found everything desirable: rebellion, nonconformity and boldness. Elvis' swiveling hips broadcast a sexuality that drove John to obsession. He also saw unbridled worldwide fame. In a televised interview with talk show host Tom Snyder in April 1975, John recalled, "One of the main reasons to get on stage is it's the quickest way of making contact, you know. You went to see those movies with Elvis or somebody in it, when we were still in Liverpool, and you'd see everybody waiting to see him, right, and I'd be waiting there, too. And they'd all scream when he came on the screen. So we thought, That's a good job."

John's infatuation with Elvis and his love of rock 'n' roll caused a separation from Mimi. At 6 years old, he had run away from his mother, but at 15 he began to run back to her. Julia's carefree and careless attitude was the complete opposite of Mimi's demeanor. While his aunt discouraged John's love for art and music, his mother encouraged him to pursue his passions. Julia played the ukulele and piano and fortified John's interest in music by buying him a guitar and teaching him to play his first chords.[8] She inspired him, encouraged his rebel behavior and laughed at everything he did. Her free-spirited attitude drew John and his friends to her house, a home filled with song.

With Julia's faith behind him, he ventured toward a life of music. He formed his first band, the Quarry Men, and played small gigs with them around Liverpool. Their most important show, arguably, was on July 6, 1957, at St. Peter's Church in Woolton. While setting up their instruments for the evening performance, he was introduced to a local 15-year-old, Paul McCartney. The two bonded, and John asked Paul to join the band. A schoolmate friend of Paul's, George Harrison, also later joined as guitar player. Life for the Quarry Men was sporadic and disorganized, but John was determined.

Then life dramatically changed again. On July 15, 1958, when John was 17 years old, his mother left Mimi's house, heading home. Crossing the street, she was struck by a car and thrown to the curb, and was pronounced dead at the scene.

The loss of Julia devastated the young musician; John later reflected, "I lost her twice."[9] In Coleman's book, John's girlfriend and future wife Cynthia Powell notes how profound an effect Julia's death had on John. "It shattered his life," she says. "He often said how terrible it was that he'd lost her just at the time she was becoming his best friend."

---

8   The Beatles Anthology, p. 11
9   Playboy, January 1981

In his book *John Lennon: In My Life*, author Pete Shotton, who was John's best friend, writes that any remaining hope for normalcy in John's life died with his mother. He felt abandoned, embittered and alone, lost all respect for the world around him, and felt no responsibility toward any adults. He became heartless and cruel in his humor. Shotton remembers him drinking so heavily he feared John would become an irrevocable drunk, and he recalls him lashing out with "horrifying cruelty" at anyone who irked him. One night he found John "stinking drunk" inside a local pub, harassing the Jewish piano player, calling out "creepy Jew-boy" and "they should have stuck you in the ovens with the rest of them." The abuse brought the piano player to tears, but no one dared approach John.

Women became a focus of John's anger, and he particularly targeted the young girls around him. He told Seaman that he "felt betrayed by all womankind" and began having violent fantasies in which he would torture them. "He would imagine crucifying women," Seaman writes, "actually nailing them to a cross, and then disemboweling them."

As for his dad, John still felt deep and bitter resentment—too painful to discuss. He rarely confided to anyone the feelings stirred by his father's abandonment and his mother's death. Powell recalled to Coleman that even she could not get John to open up about his feelings about his parents. John's sense of loss was so great that eventually he reached beyond the grave for comfort. One night, in a search for his mother, he turned to magic for answers, bringing together a group of friends to hold a séance in hope of contacting Julia in the afterworld.[10] The allure of magic was growing stronger.

When John started back at Liverpool Art College in September of 1958, biographers report that he displayed a character ever more caustic, self-absorbed and crass. He wholly abandoned a future built on academics and placed all of his hope in music. He grew obsessed with the desire to become a rich and world-famous rock star. He envisioned the life of Elvis, worshipped as a hero

---

10   Goldman, p. 78

and respected by the world and a generation. John adopted the demeanor of his tough-guy idols—Elvis, Lonnie Donegan, James Dean and Marlon Brando— and became a rebel, dressing in black, walking campus with a guitar strapped to his back, smoking cigarettes, swearing publicly and drinking alcohol. His fingers were heavily stained yellow from holding cigarettes and calloused from constantly playing guitar. He was subject to swift mood changes, and the liquor he consumed only added to his brashness, making him more obnoxious and aggressive. His manner was harsh and sarcastic, and was levied particularly at the weak—he would mock people with handicaps and disfigurements.[11]

He indulged in the edgier side of rock 'n' roll, perfecting the sound and look of Elvis and playing songs by Chuck Berry and Little Richard, the latter of whom referred to their genre as "the music of the devil." John told Coleman that he disliked the mellow ballads by artists such as Cliff Richards and other similar bands, saying, "He's so bloody Christian I can't stand him and his lot." What interested John was the pure, raw energy of rock.

He moved out of Mimi's house for the second time, into an apartment with his friend and future band mate Stuart Sutcliffe. Away from family, John was liberated to pursue girls and music. A national newspaper, *People*, featured an article about "beatnik crazies," and accompanied it with a picture of John and Stuart in their apartment. The caption stated they were "on the road to hell."

John considered success to be "getting out of Liverpool," and music would be his vehicle. What he desired most was not found in suburbia, but in the image of his idols. His disdain toward teachers and a traditional life was reflected after he became famous: "I've been proved right," he says in Hunter Davies' book *The Beatles*. "They were wrong and I was right. They're all still there, aren't they, so they must be the failures. They were all stupid teachers." In John's philosophy, those who chose jobs as educators, doctors and lawyers and chose to stay and live in Liverpool were all losers.

Moreover, he frequently shared that belief with friends. And what they noticed in John left no doubt that his fate would lie at either of two extreme

11   Davies, p. 49

ends of a spectrum. Michael Isaacson, a fellow art-college student, told Coleman: "I think if he had not become successful he may well have become more than just a wayward bum. He may well have become a really nasty piece of work. It's all hypothetical, but I fear the worst could have happened. If he hadn't become famous, his anger could have been vented into another direction. Where his energy was channeled into creative music, it would have gone into something destructive instead of creative. He was strictly an all-or-nothing kind of a guy."

John no longer merely wanted to be a rock star—he *needed* to be. So much of his angst was placed in that one dream that, psychologically, there may have been no way to backtrack without emotionally imploding. But the rock-'n'-roll life John envisioned for himself was not materializing. Following Julia's death, the Quarry Men did little for five months, and even then they only played a small, personal gig: the wedding of George Harrison's brother in December.

By 1959, John and the band were in low spirits. They briefly changed their name to Johnny and the Moondogs, and they auditioned for *The Carroll Levis Discovery Show*, a talent contest on the BBC for which they gave a decent performance but did not place.[12] In May of 1960, the band changed their name again, this time to The Silver Beetles, and secured the part-time managerial services of Allan Williams, who was otherwise occupied running a small Liverpool coffee house. Williams arranged their first official tour for that same month. The Silver Beetles—John Lennon, Paul McCartney, George Harrison, Stuart Sutcliffe and Tommy Moore—set off to Scotland as back-up to Johnny Gentle. At first the band was excited, but things did not turn out as they had fancifully envisioned. As funds for the tour diminished, so did their high expectations. With money in short supply, meals became infrequent and they began skipping out on hotel bills. Arguments continually broke out among the band members. John was particularly agitated with the whole scene as nerves frayed and tempers flared. Still, Williams kept them busy playing through June and July. Their venues often housed raucous crowds with

---

12   *The Beatles Anthology*, p. 23

reputations for violence. One particular night a young boy was kicked nearly to death while the band was playing a set.[13]

Then The Silver Beetles played at Two I's Coffee Bar in London. Attending the show was Bruno Koschmider, the owner of a club in Hamburg, West Germany. He was looking for new acts and offered The Silver Beetles a gig. The opportunity gave the band hope, but they needed a drummer to replace Moore, who'd already quit in favor of a more conventional career path.[14] So they turned to Pete Best, a drummer they knew from Liverpool's Casbah Coffee Club. They were impressed with Best's abilities, as well as his new set of drums, and they recruited him for the trip to Germany.

On August 17, 1960, they began playing a 48-night run at Hamburg's Indra Club—their first professional booking as "The Beatles." The club was located near The Reeperbahn, an urban hell, the city's red-light district, an area rife with strip clubs, sex shops, harlots, crooks, drugs and numerous drinking establishments. The band was lodged in conditions that biographer Barry Miles, in his book *Paul McCartney: Many Years from Now*, describes as "appalling." Koschmider owned a run-down former cinema around the corner from the Indra, and he allowed the Liverpool boys to sleep in its dressing rooms and to bathe in its restrooms. The Indra, previously a strip club, sported tawdry décor, heavy drapes, carpeted floors and small tables with small lights with red lampshades. On their opening night The Beatles played to only a partial house. Not long after, the club was shut down because of noise and complaints from neighbors.

The situation didn't get any more classy. The Beatles were subsequently booked for 58 nights at the Kaiserkeller, where they were soon playing to a full house of disorderly fans eager for a rowdy show. Obliging, John would launch into contortions, mimicking crippled movements and occasionally yelling to the crowd, "fucking Krauts!" and "German spassies!"[15] But far from taking offense, the German audience would respond with cheers and beers for the band. John and The Beatles took full advantage of the lifestyle, drinking and spending their money as quickly as they were paid.[16] They had at

---

13   Lewisohn, p. 20
14   Lewisohn, p. 20
15   Best, p. 42
16   Goldman, p. 106

their call many of the local girls and prostitutes, which came with its own problems—the boys were treated often for sexually transmitted diseases.[17]

The band soon ran into trouble. The police received a tip that George was only 17. West German law prohibited minors from playing in nightclubs after midnight, particularly in the seedy confines of The Reeperbahn, so the authorities informed George that he would have to leave the country. On November 17, they confiscated what little money he had earned and provided him with the balance for a plane ticket back to Liverpool. Best and Paul were not far behind. They were arrested on an alleged arson charge, and they, too, were deported.[18] With no supporting band and an expired visa, John packed up what few belongings he had and on December 10 made his way back toward Liverpool, followed by Sutcliffe a month later.

The Beatles returned home broke, dejected and dispirited, their future as a band uncertain. Davies writes that Paul did nothing but laze around the house. His father constantly pushed him to get a job, telling him several times a day, "Satan finds things for idle hands." John also spent vacant hours home alone, not even going out for two weeks. "There didn't seem anything to do," he said.

John was standing at a crossroad, discontent with his dream of rock-'n'-roll stardom. "I was so fed up I didn't bother to contact the others for a few weeks," he says in *The Beatles Anthology*. "A month is a long time at 18 or 19; I didn't know what they were doing. I just withdrew to think whether it was worth going on with. ... I thought, Is this it? Nightclubs and seedy scenes, being deported, and weird people in clubs? ... I thought hard about whether I should continue."

The situation was problematic. He was emotionally and mentally drained from years of piling disappointments—the death of his mother, the abandonment by his father, dropping out of college, two dramatically disappointing tours, and the dismal retreat of his band. He was out of a job, he was out of money. He had grown a vicious hatred for authority, he had turned his back

---

17   Brown, p. 40
18   Miles, p. 72

on religion. The dejected hopeful rock hero had little left, nothing to show for his efforts and risks, and virtually nowhere to turn. He was desperate and out of earthly options.

Yet change was only two weeks away—change that was startling in its suddenness, and profound in its magnitude. At this most critical point in his life, at the time when his fall seemed imminent and permanent, the path of John Lennon turned sharply, and almost literally overnight.

This all happened when he had nothing left to bargain with but his soul.

The Bewitchery
Of The Masses

For what shall it profit a man if he shall gain the world,
and lose his own soul?
— Mark 8:36

By the end of 1960, John Lennon's dream of becoming a rich and world-famous rock star was wholly unfulfilled. Two official tours had ended in utter disappointment. At the age of 20, he believed his days of making it big as a rock 'n' roll star were rapidly passing him by.[1]

His quest for stardom was unwavering, but how, he must have wondered, does one achieve the success he desired? What could possibly set him apart from the hundreds of bands around Liverpool at that time? If his youth was any indication of his future, he was well disillusioned. Life had offered him little to that point. His father abandoned him at 6, his mother died when he was 17; his childhood was defined largely by sadness and disappointment. Without the proper guidance and help of responsible parents, as he grew older, there was no one to attend to his cry. By 1960, John was standing at a crossroad, looking for a way to cheer his lonesome and restless life, chasing an ever-changing, transient worldly happiness. The sad remembrances of his

---

1   *The Beatles Anthology*, p. 64

past had brought him to a point where he would likely do anything and give up anything in exchange for a life as a popular musician.

Pete Best reflects John's drive in his autobiography, *Beatle! The Pete Best Story*: "I recalled once that even from the early days John had made it quite clear that he would get to the top—no matter who he had to tread on. 'One day—by one means or another,' he said more than once, 'we'll have a record in the charts. If we have to be bent or con people, then that's what we'll have to do to get there. It doesn't matter what it takes to get to the top. It might cause some heartache, but once I'm up there it'll be a different kettle of fish.' Yes, he did say '*I*' and not '*we.*' That was the real John Lennon, brilliant, amusing but ruthless."

Likewise, Beatles biographer Hunter Davis writes that John told him, "I had to be a millionaire. If I couldn't do it without being crooked, then I'd have to be crooked. I was quite prepared to do that."

At the end of 1960, something big was soon to happen, something that would change the course of music history. The rise of The Beatles was imminent—in just a few years they would become legends. And all that rapid rise began 20 years to the month before John died. If he indeed bargained his soul to the devil in exchange for two decades of fame, this is exactly when it happened.

The term "Beatlemania" was coined by the British press to describe the crowd reaction when The Beatles played the Palladium in London the evening of October 13, 1963. It would come to define the mystical response the band had world-over: the excessive emotion and enthusiasm; the chaotic crowds screaming hysterically; the frenetic behavior, uncontrollable crying, fainting and delirium. The origin of that reaction can be traced back to a single night—Tuesday, December 27, 1960—when The Beatles played the Town Hall Ballroom in Litherland, England.

On this night, The Beatles evoked a response noticeably different from anything in their past. The scene is documented in Mark Lewisohn's *The*

Complete Beatles Chronicle. "As the curtains shuffled open and Paul launched himself into Little Richard's 'Long Tall Sally,' everyone suddenly and spontaneously crushed forward to the front of the stage, swept away by the group's sheer magnetism. ... [The Beatles] were an absolute powerhouse, creating an inexplicable and unprecedented frenzy among the spellbound teenagers."

That night changed The Beatles forever. Each of them remembers the Litherland performance as the turning point in their career.

George Harrison: "We got a gig. Allan Williams put us in touch with a guy called Bob Wooler, a compere on the dance-hall circuit. He tried us out one night and put an ad in the paper: 'Direct from Hamburg: The Beatles.' And we probably looked German, too; very different from all the other groups, with our leather jackets. We looked funny and we played differently. We went down a bomb."

Paul McCartney: "We all wore black that we had picked up in Hamburg. All the Liverpool girls were saying, 'Are you from Germany?' or, 'I saw in the paper you are from Hamburg.'"

John: "Suddenly we were a wow. Mind you, 70 percent of the audience thought we were a German wow, but we didn't care about that. ... It was that evening that we really came out of our shell and let go. We stood there being cheered for the first time."[2]

Best: "Litherland was an explosion in the fortunes of The Beatles. We were playing for dancing in a hall that could accommodate some 1,500 on the dance floor at one time, but they stopped dancing when we played and surged forward in a crowd to be nearer to us, to watch every moment and above all to scream. People didn't go to a dance to scream: This was news."[3]

Attending the Litherland show was local concert promoter Brian Kelly. After seeing the crowd's reaction, he immediately began booking The Beatles to a heavy schedule for early 1961. One of the venues took the band to Liverpool's Cavern Club on Matthews Street. From their debut performance on February

2   *The Beatles Anthology*, p. 56
3   Best, p. 82

9, 1961, the number of people coming to see and hear The Beatles perform grew in a very short time. There was a sudden magnetism and fascination toward the boys from Liverpool.

In March, The Beatles left for their second trip to play in Hamburg. John's disdain for God was evident as he escalated his anti-religious behavior, mocking Christian faith and symbols. In *The Love You Make*, author Peter Brown describes how one day John donned a dog collar made of paper, cut out a paper cross and began preaching to the audience at a club. He drew a mocking picture of Jesus Christ hanging on the cross wearing a pair of bedroom slippers.

When The Beatles returned to Liverpool in July, they found the public demand for them to be greater than ever. The Cavern Club could barely contain the number of anxious fans waiting to see them play. Still, John wasn't satisfied; he deemed the success as merely local attention. If The Beatles were to achieve the scope of success he desired, then someone or something was needed to take them beyond the walls of the Cavern Club, beyond the streets of Liverpool, to the worldwide stage.

Around the same time, Brian Epstein, the manager of a local family business called North End Music Stores, began to take an interest in the local music scene. Epstein knew through sales at his store that there was a popular movement occurring around rock 'n' roll, and that The Beatles were popular up-and-comers. He also knew about the band from their prominent features in *Mersey Beat* magazine, which Epstein sold at his shop and wrote a weekly column for. The Beatles, for their part, knew of Epstein by their visits to his record store.

On November 9, 1961, Epstein went to the Cavern Club to see the band play. He later recalled in a BBC interview: "It was pretty much an eye-opener to go down into this darkened, dank, smoky cellar in the middle of the day, and to see crowds and crowds of kids watching these four young men on stage. They were rather scruffily dressed—in the nicest possible way or, I should say, in the most attractive way: black leather jackets and jeans, long hair, of course. And they had a rather untidy stage presentation, not terribly aware, and not caring very much, what they looked like. I immediately liked what I heard. They were fresh and they were honest, and they had what I thought was a 'sort of presence' and, this is a terribly vague term, 'star quality.' Whatever that is, they had it or I sensed that they had it." They smoked and ate and talked on stage, hit each other and turned their backs to the audience. But Epstein admitted they possessed a kind of magic.

Epstein began attending each of the band's performances. He was interested in their music careers, but he was also interested in John as a man. Epstein was gay and, Brown writes, obsessed with John. John was likewise possessed with Epstein, but for different reasons; he believed the music-store owner would help propel them into a wider music scene. Brown relays the story of John telling Cynthia Powell about the band's manager-to-be: "John came home to her room terribly excited. 'Our struggling days are over,' he announced. … [Epstein] was going to get them a recording contract. He knew Elvis Presley's manager, Colonel Tom Parker, and he said that The Beatles were going to be bigger than Elvis. *Bigger* than Elvis! For a while it was all Cynthia heard about."

Epstein began asking around Liverpool about the particulars of rock 'n' roll music and the business of managing a band. He learned a lot, but he was not met with flattering appraisals of The Beatles. When it came to the future Fab Four, he heard only warnings to stay away. Brown notes two particular instances of Epstein being cautioned: one was a family lawyer who tried to persuade him against managing the band, and the other was Williams, who said, "My honest opinion, Brian, is this: Don't touch them with a fucking barge pole."

But Epstein was undeterred, and ignored all advice to stay away. Whether he really just had unsubstantiated faith in this upstart local band or had some uncanny premonition or had some other unseen impetus, he seemed determined, and perhaps even predestined, to lead The Beatles—and John, in particular—to stardom.

Before officially taking those reins, he met with Aunt Mimi, who was both guarded and guarding in regard to her nephew. She told him, "It's all right for you if this group turns out to be just a flash in the pan. ... It's just a hobby for you. If it's all over in six months it won't matter to you, but what happens to them?"

Epstein replied, "It's all right, Mrs. Smith. I promise you, John will never suffer. He's the only important one. The others don't matter, but I'll always take care of John."[4]

And that he did—almost as if it was his sole purpose in life.

On December 11, 1961, with no previous experience managing a band, Epstein called The Beatles to his record store and made a proposal: He would require a percentage of their gross earnings, and in return would assume responsibility for arranging their bookings, which he guaranteed would become better organized and more prestigious and would never again pay less than £15. In addition, and most importantly, he promised to find the band a recording contract with a major British label. It was a big pitch from a small-time owner of a record shop, but it carried hope for a better life.

The room fell quiet until John finally spoke. "Right, then, Brian, manage us," he said. "Where's the contract, I'll sign it."[5] And with that, Brian Epstein became the first official manger of The Beatles.

Epstein immediately began to make adjustments with the group, from their stage presentation to the way they dressed. The next time The Beatles played at the Cavern Club, fans noticed a change in their stage presence and in the style of their music, playing arranged sets instead of unorganized jam sessions. Away from the gigs, Epstein began to sell The Beatles to everyone and anyone who would listen. He promoted them to the press, building on every minor success. He convinced Polydor records to officially release "My Bonnie"—a record the band had earlier played back-up on—under the credit of "Tony Sheridan and The Beatles," then used the record release to heavily promote the band in posters and advertisements. He constantly sought out radio and TV coverage, and in a very short time his influence was making a difference.

By early 1962, after only a few months with Epstein as manager, The Beatles were consistently playing at the Cavern Club with long lines of people

---

4   Brown, p. 63
5   Coleman, p. 247

The Beatles performing at the Cavern Club in Liverpool, England.

stretched out the door and down the sidewalk. Hundreds crammed into the small room to see them. In particular, hordes of young women came; they would gather in front of the stage, anxious to garner attention from one of the musicians. "The Cavern Club girls idolized and romanticized about The Beatles," Lewisohn writes. "At each and every performance they would desperately strive to attract the attention of one or other of the group in the hope of an acknowledgement or perhaps even a date. Two minutes before The Beatles took to the stage there would be a mass, final preening session among the girls. The dust of compact powder would clog the air, hair curlers and rollers would be removed and frantic back-combing take place."

Then Epstein began booking The Beatles to more out-of-town engagements. He advised them to have a professional attitude, including in how they presented themselves. He cleverly constructed their advertisements, often exaggerating their achievements, and in advance of their shows he provided newspapers with press releases and articles and photographs of the group. The effort was working. The Beatles landed more gigs for more fans in a further-expanding circle.

Obtaining a recording contract for the band proved much more difficult. Epstein was continually turned down. He literally walked around London, demo tape in hand, peddling The Beatles to any label that would listen. Finally the manager of a London record store pointed him to George Martin, who was searching for new talent for EMI Records' Parlophone label. Epstein quickly arranged a meeting. He gave Martin his best sales pitch, telling him The Beatles were a well-polished and practiced group that wrote their own songs and had just been voted "Best Band" in *Mersey Beat* magazine. He then played the tapes. Lewisohn writes that Martin heard "something in their music," what he defined as a "certain indefinable quality," and he expressed an interest in sometime meeting with the boys who'd recorded it.

Epstein returned to Liverpool and prepared the group for their third trip to Hamburg, this time with star treatment. The Beatles would receive a fee of £89 each, plus £44.50 per man per week. They were scheduled to play the Star-Club from April 13 to May 31. This time they traveled by plane.

The occasion was not all joyful, however. Upon the band's arrival in Germany, they were met at the airport by photographer Astrid Kirchherr. She bore bad news: Stuart Sutcliffe, one of their founding members and John's best friend, had died the night before of a brain hemorrhage. For John, it was digging up old bones and ghosts from the past. Different witnesses have offered varying accounts of his reaction: Coleman writes that John "burst into laughter." Brown writes that John "was the only dry-eyed member of the group." Best writes that John "wept like a child." Either way, his behavior in Hamburg was as coarse and avenging as ever. In the book *The Lives of John Lennon*, author Albert Goldman describes John's antics on April 20, Good Friday (the day that marks Jesus' crucifixion). John targeted his anger toward a group of Christian nuns. "The Beatles were quartered in a flat that faced the Star-Club, which was itself one door from a church and convent. On the morning of Good Friday, when the nuns stepped out of their domicile to enter the neighboring church, they were shocked to behold across the street a grotesque life-size effigy of Jesus on the cross, which John had fashioned and hung from his balcony. As the sisters gazed in astonishment at this sacrilegious display, John started pelting them with Durex condoms filled with water."

Best writes about more of John's anti-Christian behavior: "It was one of those bright May mornings with a clear blue sky, Sunday, and we were almost ready to set out for the Fish Market; a peaceful morning, with people making their way to the Catholic church that stood inexplicably alongside the Star-Club in the midst of sex and sin.

"Among them were four gentle nuns, who John espied from the flat window as we prepared to leave. 'Going for a pee,' he announced suddenly but instead of going to the bathroom, he went out on to the balcony. There, in full view of whoever might glance upwards, Lennon unzipped and sprinkled the four sisters with a mini-cloudburst out of a cloudless sky. 'Raindrops from heaven!' John gleefully yelled down at the startled nuns, who paused, then walked on serenely, well aware that this was no miracle."

Brown also writes of John's attacks against Christian worshipers: One Sunday morning, John hung a water-filled condom outside the window to taunt the Catholics on their way to church. Another time he constructed a likeness of Jesus hanging on the cross and attached an inflated condom as a penis.

If John was following the details of a traditional pact with the devil, re-affirming his pledge by rejecting Christian faith and symbols, then he was about to be well rewarded—this time, finally, with a recording contract.

Brian Epstein steered Lennon and The Beatles to unworldly success.

While The Beatles were in Germany, Epstein arranged a second meeting with Martin, set for May 9 at EMI Studios at Abbey Road in St. John's Wood. Martin was convinced to sign the band—without ever even meeting them. According to Hunter Davies, Epstein negotiated a tentative recording contract and immediately sent a telegraph to The Beatles in Germany: "Congratulations boys, EMI request recording session, please rehearse new material." He also sent the news out to the public, issued a press release and alerted *Mersey Beat* magazine. The future began to look bright for John Lennon.

News of The Beatles' recording contract spread rapidly in Liverpool. A homecoming celebration was planned at the Cavern Club for June 9, and a club-record 1,000 people attended. There was a significant movement occurring around the group, and it was all strangely happening without a hit record or wide national attention. Fans were, quite simply, awestruck. And not only were the crowds becoming larger, they were also becoming more frenzied. When the band taped a BBC radio session at the Playhouse Theatre on June 11, a large and vocal group of fans turned out to see them, and hysteria broke out in the crowd. At clubs, each arrival and departure of the band caused commotion, leaving ignorant bystanders wondering what the commotion was all about. Once when departing an event in Manchester, the group raced so franticly to their coach to avoid the crowd that they inadvertently left Best behind.

Ironically enough, they were about to do just that for real. After The Beatles' first recording session, Epstein and Martin, along with John, Paul and George, decided that Best should be replaced. It didn't take long to find a new drummer—on August 14, John telephoned Ringo Starr, who'd had moderate success with the band Rory Storm and the Hurricanes. Ringo signed on immediately and debuted as official drummer for The Beatles on August 18 at Hulme Hall in Port Sunlight, England.

In early September, Martin worked with John, Paul, George and Ringo on several potential songs for their first single, eventually choosing "Love Me Do" for the A-side, and "P.S. I Love You" as the B-side. It was released on October 5, 1962. Its movement on the charts was erratic, but eventually the song climbed to its highest point, No. 17, on December 27.

For their second single, Martin chose a John Lennon composition, "Please Please Me," and scheduled its release for January of 1963. The sound was a musical formula for success, and the song reached No. 1 on the *New Musical Express* charts on February 22. Throughout Britain, people were talking about

The Beatles, and the crowds gathering to see them started growing at a fantastic rate, resulting in the band receiving top billing for their shows. When they played the Cavern Club on February 19, long lines of fans formed two days prior to the performance.

On February 11, the group began work on their first album, which they finished in one day. Titled *Please Please Me*, it included both of their first singles along with the tracks "I Saw Her Standing There," "Do You Want To Know A Secret" and "Twist And Shout." Released on March 22, 1963, the album quickly became the best-selling in Britain and remained on top for 29 weeks, setting a record for the longest continuous run at No. 1 in the *New Musical Express* album charts.

From there, The Beatles rapidly became the epicenter of Britain's pop-rock culture. They regularly appeared on BBC radio and television, and even had their own radio series, *Pop Go The Beatles*. Their third single, "From Me To You," was released on April 11 and quickly reached No. 1, where it stayed for five weeks. They were playing sold-out shows, and the crowds' pitch was growing even more feverish. Two thousand people attended the band's concert at the Majestic Ballroom in London on April 24; 2,000 more at the Imperial Ballroom on May 11; and over 1,500 fans crowded into the City Hall in Salisbury to see them play on June 15. When The Beatles attended the annual Northwich Carnival on July 6, their mere presence caused turmoil—a reaction that was becoming common.

By mid-1963, Epstein was in the position to discriminate between venues, booking only those he deemed appropriate, and he began canceling extraneous stage and radio appearances. The band was outgrowing every club they'd played, even at home. Thus, on July 21, after nearly 300 appearances spanning two and a half years, the Cavern Club began selling tickets for its last Beatles show—they simply could no longer contain the public's demand for the band. Tickets went on sale at 1:30 p.m. and were sold out by 2 o'clock.

On August 23, The Beatles released their fourth single, "She Loves You," and within a few weeks it was No. 1, where it stayed for a month. The record sold 1.3 million copies in Great Britain by the end of the year and became 1963's best-selling single.

As another measure of their growing success, The Beatles were booked to play the London Palladium on October 13, a premium engagement at the ultimate British performance venue of the time. *Val Parnell's Sunday Night at The London Palladium* was the top-rated television program in England. The Beatles were top-billed, thousands of fans turned up at the theater to see them, and an estimated 15 million more tuned in to watch on television. Davies describes the scene: "Argyll Street, where the Palladium is situated, was besieged by fans all day long. Newspapermen started arriving once the stories of the crowds got round. The stage door was blocked by fans, mountains of presents, and piles of telegrams. Inside it was almost impossible to rehearse for the continual screams of the thousands of fans chanting outside in the streets." When The Beatles took the stage, the sound of their music could barely be heard over the screaming fans; at one point, writes Lewisohn, as Paul was trying to introduce a song, John began yelling "Shut up!" to the crowd.

A few days after the Palladium performance, it was announced that The Beatles were invited to play at the Royal Variety Show in front of the Queen Mother, Princess Margaret and Lord Snowdon. The show was broadcast across Britain by radio and television. The fame The Beatles were now achieving was unprecedented, as was the behavior of the fans. Epstein no longer allowed the boys to play concerts in open auditoriums, but instead chose halls with fixed seating, allowing for better crowd control and greater safety for the band.

Another "first" was looming. In October, The Beatles left Great Britain for a tour of Sweden, and upon returning home at the end of the month, they received their initial "airport reception." People began arriving at Heathrow early in the morning and by the time The Beatles landed, nearly 10,000 cheering fans were there to greet them.

The band went back into the studio to complete work on their second album, *With The Beatles* (titled *Meet The Beatles* in the U.S.). Released on November 22, the record reached No. 1 on the charts in just five days—taking the spot from *Please Please Me*—and remained on top for 21 weeks, selling over a million copies in Britain.

By the end of 1963, the United Kingdom was witnessing a cultural phenomenon like never seen before. When The Beatles played the Empire Theatre in Liverpool on December 7, the BBC broadcast was seen by 23 million people. The band had become such staples on radio and television—with documentary stories dedicated entirely to their success—that Brits began referring to the BBC as "Beatles Broadcasting Company." Interviews with the band were held before and after every concert. The news footage was always the same: chaos created by anxious fans. Additionally, the band's playing fee had grown to £1,000.

John was thrilled with their quick fame, but, Shotton writes, he still deemed the British success as merely local attention, and therefore inadequate to fulfill his larger ambition. Liverpool, London and all of Great Britain weren't enough—John wanted the world. After the Empire Theater concert, he called Shotton and asked to meet. When Shotton arrived, he found John digging through a cabinet of his personal belongings, collecting old books and papers he said he wanted to take with him to London. Shotton writes that John talked excessively about his desire for riches and world fame, and his ambition to become a legend. He talked about the recent success of the band, the "screaming mobs, the getaway limousines … the celebrities they were meeting—and the girls they were screwing—in the dressing rooms." It was a small taste of the things John wanted most.

Shotton also describes how, that night, John went on and on about America. "'America, America, America,' he repeated, almost like an incantation."

"Now if I could just get America," John told Shotton, "I've got the fucking world!"

Webster's Third New International Dictionary defines "incantation" as "a use of spells or verbal charms spoken or sung as a part of a ritual of magic." In just a few short weeks, John Lennon's incantation was answered; his magic produced a result. Epstein received a call from Ed Sullivan.

The Beatles suddenly took off in America. On January 17, 1964, they were informed that "I Want to Hold Your Hand" had reached the No. 1 spot on the U.S. charts, jumping from No. 43 to the top in one week. The single sold 250,000 copies in just a couple of days, and over 1 million within a few weeks. At one point in New York City alone, writes Lewisohn, it was selling 10,000 copies an hour. When the album *Meet The Beatles* went on sale in the U.S. on January 20, it sold 750,000 copies in the first week. All of this happened before The Beatles even set foot in the country.

That first trip, already arranged, was scheduled for less than a month later. They could never have planned such a fortuitously timely arrival. The confluence of circumstances seemed almost unavoidable, almost inescapable, almost preordained. Even The Beatles were awed. "All these forces started working so that when we landed in the U.S. the record was No. 1," George says in *The Beatles Anthology*. "We were booked five months ahead and you can't plan that kind of thing."

Paul: "'From Me To You' was released—a flop in America. 'She Loves You'—a big hit in England—big No. 1 in England—a flop in the U.S.A. 'Please Please Me' released over there—flop. Nothing until 'I Want To Hold Your Hand.'"[6]

Ringo: "Things used to fall right for us as a band. We couldn't stop it. The gods were on our side."

John: "It was just out of the dark. That's the truth: it was so out of the dark, we were knocked out."

Epstein: "We knew that America would make us or break us as world stars. In fact she made us."[7]

On February 7, 1964, The Beatles set off for John F. Kennedy International Airport in New York City. All day radio stations in New York were announcing updates of the band's progress toward the U.S., and as the hours passed the number of fans at the airport grew. By the time The Beatles arrived, 3,000 people covered the international arrival deck, singing and holding signs of welcome. The Associated Press described the airport reception as "a teen-age storm."

6   *The Beatles Anthology*, p. 115
7   *The Beatles Anthology*, p. 115-116

At 1:20 p.m., the plane touched down. "There were millions of kids at the airport, which nobody had expected," Paul McCartney says in *Anthology*. "We heard about it in mid-air. There were journalists on the plane, and the pilot had rang ahead and said, 'Tell the boys there's a big crowd waiting for them.' We thought, Wow! God, we have really made it."

From the moment The Beatles landed in New York, journalists, photographers, radio stations and television news crews covered their every move. Hundreds of reporters clamored for their attention, if only for a few seconds, in person, by phone, by any means possible. The press conference at Kennedy was broadcast live. Upon leaving the airport, each Beatle was given their own limousine. Local TV and radio interrupted regularly scheduled programs to report on the band's movement. New Yorkers were given live updated reports of The Beatles' motorcade. "I remember," Paul continues, "the great moment of getting into the limo and putting on the radio, and hearing a running commentary on *us*; 'They have just left the airport and are coming towards New York City. ...' It was like a dream. The greatest fantasy ever." Filmmakers David and Albert Maysles documented the visit, footage of which was played on national British television. Video shows the motorcade traveling through streets of Manhattan lined with screaming fans. When The Beatles arrived at the Plaza Hotel near Central Park, it was mobbed with thousands of people. The elite hotel was not prepared for the overwhelming response, and as the day went on the crowds grew even larger. Eventually police had to block off parts of Fifth Avenue to maintain order. The Beatles spent most of their time in their rooms, unable to leave because of the commotion outside. From there they filmed video clips and conducted live telephone interviews with local radio stations. BBC radio also broadcast telephone conversations with The Beatles from the Plaza Hotel, and claimed that 20 percent of the population of Great Britain listened.

The next day photographers followed Paul, Ringo and John through Central Park, while George stayed at the hotel sick with the flu. One resulting, foreseeing picture shows the three Beatles on a bridge; in the background stands the Dakota apartment building, site of John's violent death 16 years later.

The Beatles were scheduled to perform live on the nationally televised *Ed Sullivan Show* on February 9. The program had previously premiered many of the world's greatest entertainers, including Elvis Presley, but The Beatles' appearance was like nothing seen before. According to the *Washington Post*, 50,000 people applied for 700 tickets to the show. The Beatles performed five songs: "All My Loving," "Till There Was You," "She Loves You," "I Saw Her Standing There" and "I Want To Hold Your Hand." An estimated 73 million Americans viewed the broadcast, shattering the previous world record for the largest-ever television audience.

Ed Sullivan later commented, "I have never seen any scenes to compare with the bedlam that was occasioned by their debut [on the show]. Broadway was jammed with people for almost eight blocks. They screamed, yelled, and stopped traffic. It was indescribable. And on that same bill with them were the comedian Frank Gorshin, Tessy O'Shay and the youngsters from the Broadway hit of the day, *Oliver!* There has never been anything like it in show business, and the New York City police were very happy it didn't and wouldn't happen [in New York] again."[8]

John and The Beatles now had the attention of America. Beatlemania was on full display in a whole new arena. The band's first live concert in the U.S.—at the Washington (D.C.) Coliseum, just two days after the *Ed Sullivan* appearance—sold out. In what was fast becoming a trend, the audience screamed with such intensity that many couldn't even hear the music.

Following the performance, The Beatles were invited to a party at the British Embassy. The crowd there was also excited to see them, but not in as quite an acceptable way. The visit did not go well, as Brown recounts in *The Love You Make*. "The party crowd converged on the boys demanding they sign autographs," Brown writes. "One of the guests, watching John sign, remarked sotto voice, 'Look, he can actually write!'" John, insulted, but not punching the man (as the band expected), stopped giving autographs until an embassy

---

The Beatles—Paul McCartney, John Lennon, George Harrison and Ringo Starr—could not explain the reason for becoming an unparalleled and spell-binding cultural and social phenomenon.

official shoved a piece of paper under his nose and said, "You'll sign this and like it." The band briefly complied until another guest, without asking, reached toward Ringo with a pair of cuticle scissors and cut off a lock of his hair. Infuriated, The Beatles promptly left. Afterward Epstein vowed to never again allow the band to be used at any government function. "No diplomat, no royalty, no president would ever have The Beatles at their beck and call for their amusement," Brown writes. It would be their first and last embassy visit, but not their last trouble with a government.

The boys flew back to New York City for two sold-out 25-minute performances at Carnegie Hall. Afterward Epstein walked with Sid Bernstein, promoter of the shows, through the streets of Manhattan, talking about The Beatles. They stopped in front of Madison Square Garden and Bernstein said he had no doubt the band could fill the hall. Epstein had a bigger mission. "We'll book football stadiums," he replied. "We'll fill the largest arenas in the world."[9]

9   Brown, p. 113

From New York The Beatles flew to Miami for their second appearance on *The Ed Sullivan Show* in front of a live audience of 3,500 and an estimated 70 million U.S. television viewers. Then, on February 22, they returned home and were again welcomed by thousands of fans at Heathrow Airport.

In late February, The Beatles returned to the studio to record songs for their third album, *A Hard Day's Night*, and then began filming their first full-length movie of the same title. In mid-March their sixth single, "Can't Buy Me Love," topped the charts everywhere it was released. In the U.S., it sold more than 2 million copies in one week, earning Gold Disc designation on the day it was issued, an unprecedented achievement. In Britain, advance orders alone topped 1 million. In April, *Billboard* magazine's charts listed The Beatles at Nos. 1, 2, 3, 4 and 5 for singles ("Can't Buy Me Love," "Twist and Shout," "She Loves You," "I Want to Hold Your Hand," and "Please Please Me"), and Nos. 1 and 2 for albums (*Meet the Beatles* and *Introducing ... the Beatles*, the latter a U.S. version of *Please Please Me*). No artist before or since has achieved even close to that level of chart status.

After finishing filming *A Hard Day's Night*, The Beatles embarked on a 27-day world tour that included stops in Denmark, The Netherlands, Hong Kong, Australia and New Zealand. The international crowds were just as fanatic as America's and Britain's. Greetings at airports were now routine, each including a nationally televised press conference and an audience question-and-answer session. In Holland, the band had to leave in the middle of a performance because eager fans were trying to join them on stage. In Amsterdam, The Beatles took a canal trip, and the jaunt was transmitted to a national TV network. Their two live performances in The Netherlands were filmed by television and news crews.

But nothing could prepare them for what was waiting Down Under. When their plane made an *unscheduled* stopover in Darwin, Australia, at 2:30 a.m., 400 fans were at the airport to greet them. The band arrived in Sydney on June 11 during a torrential rainstorm, but still a packed airport of uproarious fans waited to greet them there, as well. Newspaper headlines reported Beatlemania and mass hysteria; news reels show their motorcade traveling through massive, delirious crowds lining the streets. "The Beatles' reception in Australia was, if anything, more riotous than their American welcome four months previously," Lewisohn writes. "Manic scenes preceded and then accompanied their every move throughout the tour. Many were hurt in the 24-hour-a-day chaos, and The Beatles ... were pulled and pushed, shoved, grabbed and screamed at from close proximity throughout the entire trip."

Lewisohn further notes that an estimated 300,000 people pooled outside the band's hotel in Adelaide. United Press International reported that "monumental traffic jams [occurred in the city] when thousands of cars converged on the highway leading to the airport," and that many teenagers abandoned their cars and climbed roadside trees so they could see The Beatles' convoy.

When the band arrived in Melbourne, 5,000 people stood in freezing temperatures to greet them. When The Beatles got into the city, pandemonium ensued. Three hundred policemen were quickly overwhelmed by 250,000 fans, prompting authorities to call in 100 soldiers and sailors to help contain the crowd. Later, civilian volunteers had to be recruited to buttress the official security forces. They all linked arms to try to hold back the masses, but the lines broke quickly. Fans were trampled underfoot and against steel barriers, and women fainted and were passed over the crowd to safety. Ambulances were sent screaming away one after another, carrying 100 injured citizens to hospitals by the end of the day. No one was killed, a fact the police attributed to a miracle.[10]

Lewisohn writes that The Beatles likened the enormous Australian crowds to the type Hitler had attracted in Germany, and John responded accordingly: In one video, he is clearly seen performing a Nazi salute to the masses.

The trip to Australia grossed over £200,000 for The Beatles, while their concerts attracted 200,000 fans. In *Anthology* John says, "Australia was a high moment. ... There were more people that came to see us there than anywhere. I think the whole of Australia was there. We must have seen a million people before they let us go."

The Beatles returned to London for the July 6 world premiere of *A Hard Day's Night*. Piccadilly Circus and the surrounding streets were lined with po-

---

10   United Press International, June 15, 1964

licemen in an effort to contain the thousands of fans who were there to greet the band. Four days later, the scene was even bigger for their homecoming in Liverpool. "It was incredible, because people were lining the streets that we'd known as children, that we'd taken the bus down, or walked down. We'd been to the cinema with girls down these streets. And here we were now with thousands of people—for us," Paul says in *Anthology*. "We ended up at Liverpool Town Hall on the balcony, with throngs of people—200,000, in fact—all out there between the Town Hall and the Cavern." In video clips, John can once again be seen performing the Nazi salute.

The movie *A Hard Day's Night* opened to rave reviews, and the accompanying album soared to the top of the charts around the world. Released in Britain on July 10, the record rose to No. 1 in five days and remained there for 21 weeks; released in the U.S. on June 26, it rose to No. 1 by late July and stayed there for 14 weeks. It sold 2 million copies by October 1964.

In mid-August, The Beatles left England for their first full tour of the U.S. They arrived in San Francisco International Airport and were greeted by 9,000 screaming teenagers. Their first concert appearance was in San Francisco's Cow Palace on August 18, which kicked off an itinerary of 32 shows at 26 venues in 24 cities in 34 days. Scenes of rampage and Beatlemania were evident from the beginning to the end of the tour. It was now commonplace for the band to spend the majority of their time on planes, in hotels, in limousines and in press conferences while being smuggled in and out of towns and arenas.

They were also being offered increasingly large sums of money to play. Lewisohn describes a deal that displays how much the band was in demand: "During the course of The Beatles' concert in San Francisco, Brian Epstein was visited by Charles O. Finley, the millionaire owner and president of the Kansas City Athletics baseball team. Finley was disappointed that Kansas City hadn't been included in the tour itinerary and had vowed to the city that he would somehow get The Beatles to play there. He offered Brian Epstein first $50,000 and then $100,000 for one concert but was refused both times. It could only be arranged for 17 September but this was designated as a rest day to enable The Beatles to visit New Orleans. But Finley was persistent, and eventually in Los Angeles, came his breakthrough: He tore up the $100,000 check in Epstein's face, tossed it into an ashtray and wrote out another for $150,000, a record fee paid in America for one show. Epstein told Finley to wait a moment while he talked it over with 'the boys.' The boys were in the middle of another interminable card game when Epstein walked in and showed them the check. 'What do you want to do about it?' he asked. With the other three nodding in agreement, John—hardly bothering to look up—simply shrugged his shoulders and replied, 'We'll do whatever you want.' Epstein went back to Finley and accepted. For that one night The Beatles reluctantly earned $4,838 per minute. It was, remember, just 13 months after they had last played at the Cavern Club."

And the commerce surrounding The Beatles didn't end when they left town. Lewisohn writes: "After The Beatles left Kansas City, the manager of their hotel sold all of their bed linen—16 sheets and eight pillow-slips—to two Chicago businessmen for $750. Unlaundered, it was then cut into three-inch squares, mounted on a card and sold with a legal affidavit at $10 at a time. The towels used by The Beatles to mop their faces immediately after their Hollywood Bowl concert on 23 August were similarly cut into portions and sold. In New York City, cans of 'Beatle Breath' were on sale and requests were received for The Beatles' bathwater and used shaving foam."

All this unprecedented success and the surrounding mania prompted an oft-repeated question amongst the public and the media: Why? The Beatles weren't just a successful rock band, they were an unparalleled cultural and social phenomenon. What could possibly precipitate such a quick rise to world fame and such a spellbinding effect on the masses? The question was prevalent even in The Beatles' press conferences:

New York City, February 7
Q: "What do you think your music does for these people?"

Washington, D.C., February 11
Q: "Tell me this—why do you think you're so popular all of a sudden?"

Melbourne, Australia, June 14

Q: "In view of the fact that you've had so much experience now with crowd hysteria, are you still at a loss to put your finger on the reason why?"

Q: "Can we ask you to amplify the point, how this hysteria generates? Nobody seems to be able to put their finger on a reason why. It seems to be a combination of things. What do you believe it is?"

New York City, August 28

Q: "As seriously as you can, how do you account for the type of reception you get?"

Paul: "We can't account for it, you know. We …"

Q: "It's been going on for quite a few months now. You must have some ideas about why people like you."

Chicago, September 5

Q: "Will you tell us why you think you are so popular?"

John: "We don't think about it. We get asked that, you know—somebody asks us that every day, and we've no answer."

Lennon had no answer—or no answer that he wanted to share. Others, at least metaphorically, began to allude to "devilish" behavior.

The Seattle Times asked Dr. Bernard Seibel, a child guidance expert for the state of Washington, to attend a Beatles concert and report on the demeanor of the fans. "The hysteria and loss of control go far beyond the impact of the music," Seibel writes. "Many of those present became frantic, hostile, uncontrolled, screaming, unrecognizable beings. … The externals are terrifying. Normally recognizable girls behaved as if possessed by some demonic urge. … Why do the kids scream, faint, gyrate and in general look like a primeval, protoplasmic upheaval and go into ecstatic convulsions? … Regardless of the causes or reasons for the behavior of these youngsters, it had the impact of an unholy bedlam."

Backstage, another phenomenon was occurring: The Beatles were being deified. People began to perceive in them supernatural healing powers.

Ringo: "Crippled people were constantly being brought backstage to be touched by 'a Beatle,' and it was very strange. ... There were some really bad cases, God help them ... kids with little broken bodies, and no arms, no legs and little feet."

George: "We were only trying to play rock 'n' roll and they'd be wheeling them in, not just in wheelchairs but sometimes in oxygen tents. What did they think that we would be able to do? ... We'd come out of the band room to go to the stage and we'd be fighting our way through all these poor unfortunate people. John didn't like it."

John: "Wherever we went on tour, there were always a few seats laid aside for cripples and people in wheelchairs. ... And it's always the mother or nurse pushing them on you. They would push these people at you like you were Christ, as if there were some aura about you that would rub off on them. ... It seemed that we were just surrounded by cripples and blind people all the time, and when we would go through corridors they would all be touching us. It was horrifying."[11]

By late 1964, John Lennon's monumental success may have seemed bittersweet. While achievement should have brought happiness, he instead appeared tormented. The Beatles returned to Great Britain from their trips to America and Australia, and they promptly began recording new material. And the songs were starting to sound different. The writing from John, in particular, began to become introspective, revealing a darker side that suggested inner trouble and misplaced joy. It was evident that something in his attitude had changed. The first song he wrote in the new studio sessions was "Baby's in Black," followed by "I'm a Loser." Even the title of the new album perhaps communicated a message: *Beatles for Sale*. But the price for fame may had already been negotiated.

---

11   *The Beatles Anthology*, p. 142-143

"I Feel Fine" was distributed as a single in late November and sold millions of copies, broke sales records, and reached No. 1 in the charts—reproducing, yet again, what had become the norm for a Beatles release. *Beatles for Sale* was released on December 4—the band's fourth album in 21 months. It reached, of course, No. 1.

It seemed nothing could go wrong.

In early 1965, The Beatles began work on another album and film, each titled *Help!*, each of which contained the John Lennon-penned song of the same title. John had the world at his feet, fame and wealth, and the adulation of innumerable women, and yet he was crying for help. In a short time, he had gone from singing "please please me" to "please, please help me."

Still, the adulation only continued to grow. On April 9, The Beatles received a Radio Caroline Bell Award. On April 11, they were announced as *New Musical Express'* 1964-'65 annual poll winner. On April 28, comedian Peter Sellers visited the *Help!* film set to present The Beatles with a Grammy Award for Best Performance by a Vocal Group, for "A Hard Day's Night." On June 12, the band was notified that they would be awarded as Members of the Most Honorable Order of the British Empire.

It was during this time The Beatles started using LSD. According to *Anthology*, their first experience with the mind-altering drug was not deliberate—a friend slipped it in their coffee. But they would knowingly take the drug many times hence. For The Beatles, LSD opened a world of self-reflection; it brought them in touch with their conscience. George explains in *Anthology* that LSD gave him awareness, and what he saw in John left him bothered. He sensed his band mate was having problems. "In a way, like psychiatry, acid could undo a lot—it was *so* powerful you could just *see*," George says in the book. "We didn't really realize the extent to which John was screwed up. ... As a kid, I didn't think, 'Oh well, it's because his dad left home and his mother died,' which in reality probably did leave an incredible scar. ... [Later] I realized he was even more screwed up than I thought."

In late June, The Beatles began another world tour that eventually brought them to what many still consider the pinnacle of their playing career: Shea Stadium in New York City, August 15, 1965. It was the first outdoor rock 'n' roll show in a large arena; it emerged as a defining moment in music history, a main event and the biggest concert of their careers. The degree of fan hysteria was extraordinary, even for The Beatles.

In early evening, they left Manhattan's Warwick Hotel by limousine. Police blocked off all roads for the motorcade, and the band was whisked through intersections and traffic lights. They arrived at a waterfront heliport and boarded a helicopter that flew them to the roof of a World's Fair building in Queens. From there, they rode in an armored Wells Fargo truck to Shea Stadium. Upon arrival, they were immediately mobbed by frenzied fans who began rocking and banging the sides of the vehicle.

At 9:16 p.m., The Beatles ran through a tunnel leading to the stadium field. From the moment they first appeared, the screams were continuous. Most of the 55,600 in attendance couldn't even hear the music, and The Beatles could barely hear it either.

Officials had created a space buffer between the crowd and the band. The stage was located on the baseball diamond at second base, and scores of police roamed the more than 100 feet of grass between the fans and The Beatles. An 8-foot-high security fence loomed at the edge of the stands to prevent people from accessing the field; kids could be seen climbing the fence throughout the show, and those who got onto the field were quickly tackled and carried off by police officers. Any special movement made by the band was followed by even more intense screaming. The Beatles were standing at the center of a storm, a madness that seemed indefinable and superhuman. Their set list for the night: "Twist and Shout," "She's a Woman," "I Feel Fine," "Dizzy Miss Lizzy," "Ticket to Ride," "Everybody's Trying to be My Baby," "Can't Buy Me Love," "Baby's in Black," "Act Naturally," "A Hard Day's Night," "Help!" and "I'm Down."

And there stood John Lennon, showered with accolades. At the age of 24, he was witnessing the magnitude of his achievement on display in front of him. But while he should have been standing at the microphone feeling

joyous, he instead seemed uneasy, struggling at center-stage. A quiet personal struggle may have finally begun to be outwardly expressed. The screams
from the crowd seemed to be going to his core. He appeared disquieted, he
was perspiring, and his hair was matted to his forehead and falling into his
eyes, which appeared guarded and bedeviled. A red glow from the stage lights
bathed his face, and he appeared haunted. It was an almost surreal, supernatural moment.

The world had never seen such a display of overwhelming devotion toward a rock 'n' roll band. John was later widely quoted as describing the
noise as "louder than God." Why did he choose that analogy? Was he
just reaching for profound effect, or was religion on his mind? The latter
wouldn't be surprising, and could certainly cause the strange behavior he
began to exhibit during the show. Was the price of his fame weighing heavy
on his shoulders, weighing heavy on his soul? John may have been realizing
that this was the apex, the answer to his dark wishes and desires, and that
his rapid assent to success would soon bear a spiritual cost. He appeared
noticeably shaken, at one point holding his out-stretched hands toward the
sky as if asking, "What's happening?" And he was standing in front of the
world singing "help." After the show, John told promoter Bernstein, "I saw
the top of the mountain."[12]

In *Anthology*, Ringo comments on John's behavior during the Shea Stadium performance: "It was very big and very strange. I felt that on that show
John cracked up. He went mad, not mentally ill, but he just got crazy. He was
playing the piano with his elbows and it was really strange."

The attendance was a world record for a pop concert. The band earned
$160,000 of the $304,000 gross receipts, a world-record amount. But most
significantly, a page was turned. August 15, 1965, is when The Beatles stopped
being teen pop stars and became legends. A page was turned for John, too;
his writing would become even deeper and more reflective, his words would
become more controversial, his time on the road would become more turbu-
lent. Moreover, viewed in retrospect, clues began to crop up—clues that there

---

12   *The New York Times*, Aug. 15, 2000

was more to John's darker mood than just stress or creative growing pains. Deliberately or not, he began to reveal, in slivers of insight, that he often ruminated on something sinister.

The 1965 tour wore on for another two weeks. They played more shows, made more money, were mobbed by more crazed fans. Then at the end of summer, they flew home to England and quickly began work on another album.

John's writing grew even more introspective, reflecting on his personal life and suggesting inner conflicts. During this time he penned "Run For Your Life," about vengeful jealousy; "Norwegian Wood (This Bird Has Flown)," about an affair he was having; "In My Life," a sobering reminiscence that remains one of his most autobiographical songs; and "Nowhere Man," the first Beatles composition not about love, written as a self-critical lament. His mates noticed the change; they knew that John's "Nowhere Man" lyrics were not meaningless. Paul says in a December 1984 *Playboy* interview, "I think at that point, he was a bit … wondering where he was going. … I was starting to worry about him."

One subject particularly on John's mind at that time was religion, and some of those thoughts are revealed in the symbolism of the song "Girl," which he wrote during those same sessions. In the lyrics, as he told *Rolling Stone* in 1970, John expresses the conflict he was having with religion. He explained that one stanza dealt with the "Catholic/Christian concept [that says] be tortured and you'll be alright."

> *Was she told when she was young*
> *that pain would lead to pleasure?*
> *Did she understand it when they said*
> *that a man must break his back*
> *to earn his day of leisure?*
> *Will she still believe it when he's dead?*

Using rather benign lyrics, John was rejecting the belief that suffering must precede happiness. As noted by author Steve Turner in *A Hard Day's Write*, John may have been thinking about the Bible book Genesis. In that book, Adam and Eve's disobedience—prompted by temptation from Satan—leads to God saying to Eve, "With pain you will give birth to children," and to Adam, "Cursed is the ground because of you; through painful toil you will eat of it all the days of your life."

"Christianity, and in particular Jesus Christ, seemed to bother John," Turner writes. "At the time of writing 'Girl,' he was avidly reading books about religion, a subject that preoccupied him until his death."

Of further interest is the album's name. Though released as *Rubber Soul*, the original working title was *The Magic Circle*.[13] Magic circles have been used by conjurers for centuries. According to *A Dictionary of Religion and Ethics*, "From primitive times a circle drawn about a person has been considered a means of supernatural defense. ... By convergence of ideas, rings, girdles, head-bands and bracelets acquired a magical power to keep in or to keep out spirit influences. In medieval Europe the magic circle was ... inscribed with a great variety of mysterious signs and used as a talisman or, drawn on the ground, as a vantage point from which safely to call up and wrest knowledge from spirits."

The Beatles' 1965 album *Rubber Soul* had an original working title of *The Magic Circle*. It is speculated that the band is depicted looking into a grave with John being the only one of the four looking straight down, perhaps forecasting his fate.

The forms of magic circles vary, but many have common elements of written words and intersecting lines. Most historical research reveals that magic circles have been used by different groups for different purposes ranging from the conjuring of demons and spirits to protection from the same. Either way, circles are thought to have power and energy. They can be symbolic of a cycle

13   Dowlding, p. 113

of existence, of returning to source, of finding your way home. They also represent eternity, for a circle has neither visible beginning nor end. And regardless of their intended use—for good or evil, for prayer or invocation—magic circles are certainly one of the most basic devices in the magical arts. And one was meant to be the prominent symbol of John's next album.

Even once changed to *Rubber Soul*, the cover concept still hinted at the possible past and future of John Lennon. The title logo is designed in the shape of an upside-down heart; the believers of the Paul-is-Dead rumor would later widely believe the logo to indicate that a "false soul" or "deceived heart" was among the group. Many have also agreed that the photo depicts what appears to be The Beatles staring downward into an open grave. Paul, George and Ringo are looking away from the focal point (the grave), whereas John is staring directly into it—indicating that he is the person with the compromised soul, and the person who would one day fill its space.

More Popular Than Jesus

Jesus, a garlic-eating, stinking little yellow,
greasy fascist bastard catholic Spaniard.
— John Lennon

For the first three months of 1966, The Beatles were on holiday. John Lennon spent his time lounging at his Kenwood estate in Weybridge, England. In January, he gave an interview with Maureen Cleave for the *London Evening Standard*, in which he describes himself as "famous and loaded" and the laziest person in England. "I don't mind writing or reading or watching or speaking," he said, "but sex is the only physical thing I can be bothered with any more."

The article also contains a handful of quotes about his views on religion, including this: "Christianity will go. It will vanish and shrink. I needn't argue about that; I'm right and I will be proved right. We're more popular than Jesus now; I don't know which will go first—rock 'n' roll or Christianity. Jesus was all right but his disciples were thick and ordinary. It's them twisting it that ruins it for me."

When published in England in March, the article received little reaction, and little attention. That would change.

61

According to Pete Shotton, by early 1966 John was taking a variety of drugs on a daily basis. "They quite literally used to eat it like candy," Shotton writes. "He used to appear in my bedroom every morning with a breakfast tray containing a cup of tea and a tab of acid." The daily trips started influencing John's music and lyrics, a fact apparent when The Beatles returned to the recording studio in April to start work on a new album, *Revolver*. His songs began to express thoughts about death and the afterlife and his concerns about the future, and he started using looped tracks and backward music and voices in compositions (such as what's heard in "Rain" and "Tomorrow Never Knows").

The band's publicity photos took a bizarre turn, as well. On June 15, Capitol Records, their American label, released the album *Yesterday and Today* in the U.S. and Canada. On the cover, The Beatles were pictured smiling in white butcher's coats amongst pieces of baby dolls—with heads, legs, and arms removed from the bodies—intermingled with pieces of real raw meat that hung over their shoulders and laps. The image was one of massacre and sacrifice. It would come to be known as "the butcher cover."

Not surprisingly, retailers were appalled. Advance copies generated complaints from store managers and radio disc jockeys, prompting Capitol to promptly recall the album—750,000 copies of which had already been printed. The company destroyed some of the offending sleeves, but merely covered others with new art and re-shipped them. Still, news of the photo was out, and it raised numerous questions. In a letter responding to the complaints, the label defended the original cover as merely "'pop art' satire" that was "subject to misinterpretation." Pete Johnson of the *Los Angeles Times* responded: "Misinterpretation is a mild description of what would probably ensue when the 13-year-olds began trotting into kitchens to show their harried mothers what their photogenic idols were up to. ... How can The Beatles associate themselves with infanticide? They will have all the teenagers killing off their tiny siblings."

The practice of sacrificing human beings is unfortunately well established throughout history, and it continues in the world as a ritual form of worship in radical, cultish religions that are, quite obviously, dark in nature. Even today the media reports on sadistic murders with occult overtones,

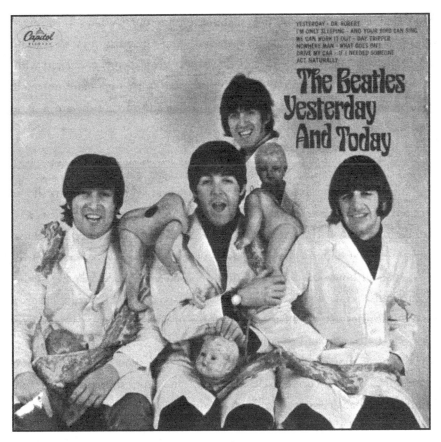

John Lennon lobbied for the use of the controversial "infanticide" album cover for *Yesterday and Today.*

murders involving ritual mutilation, dismemberment and cannibalism. But the most reviling sacrifice to Satan involves the killing of young, innocent children—infanticide.

Was that type of portrayal the impetus behind The Beatles' "butcher cover"? They have never admitted or alluded to that being true. In fact, they didn't even all like the idea of the photo. "I thought it was gross, and I also thought it was stupid," George Harrison says in *The Beatles Anthology.*

The Beatle who ardently lobbied for releasing the gruesome cover was John. "I don't like being locked in to one game all the time, and there we were supposed to be sort of angels," he says in *Anthology.* "I wanted to show that we were aware of life, and I really was pushing for that album cover. I would say I was a lot of the force behind it going out." What's most interesting about his words is that he specifically did not want to be seen as an angel; he was making an effort to move away from being associated with a benevolent creature close to God. It was yet another step—and not such a small one—in a journey that moved further and further toward a dark destination.

In June of 1966, The Beatles started another world tour. Beatlemania shone on, but was starting to grow reckless and unsafe. As a result, security grew larger and tighter. The band traveled to Japan for a scheduled five-show performance at Nippon Budokan Hall in the center of Tokyo. Prior to their visit, a small but vocal demonstration opposed The Beatles playing at the hall because some considered the location sacred. Death threats ensued, and authorities assembled a security force of 35,000, the largest ever to protect The Beatles and to control Beatles-related mayhem. The only time the band was allowed to leave the hotel was for their shows, after which they were immediately escorted back. They were allowed to shop, but only with mobile merchants: A stream of local peddlers was invited to their rooms to sell goods. The group's daily schedule was prearranged and planned down to the minute.[1] Then upon leaving the country, The Beatles were spared the usual airport sendoff by young fans. According to a Reuters report, police stopped 80 cars from following the band's motorcade and cleared the terminal of over 2,000 teenagers, many of whom were "caught hiding in toilets and a warehouse."

From Japan, The Beatles headed to the Philippines. The scene around them grew crazier still.

They arrived on July 3 and were met on the runway by a car of armed guards who whisked them away immediately—sans luggage, sans entourage, sans management. They were transported to a yacht miles offshore in Manila Harbor, then after Brian Epstein's intervention, to a downtown

---

1   *The Beatles Anthology*, p. 215-216

hotel. Things were a bit more under control—for the moment. But the following morning, The Beatles watched their hotel-room TV as a news commentator was shown at the Presidential Palace—waiting for *their* arrival. It was thought the band was to meet with First Lady Imelda Marcos, her three kids and a group of 300 other women and children. But The Beatles had made no such promise or plans, and, obviously, never showed up. Imelda and others stood waiting at the palace for over half an hour. The public viewed the event as a snub of the first family, which quickly led to chaos; they were not happy, and they rebelled. That evening the band gave two performances as scheduled, attended by a reported 75,000 fans—half of what had been expected, according to the Associated Press. The next morning the hotel staff failed to serve them breakfast. When the band checked out they were made to carry their own luggage. Outside the hotel, upset locals yelled at them.[2] When The Beatles arrived at the airport the situation deteriorated even more. According to an AP report, the band was denied their usual VIP privileges and protective security forces were cancelled. The airport manager turned off power to the escalators, no porters were in sight and The Beatles again had to carry their own bags. As they filled out their exit forms, a mad and vocal group of people began harassing them, booing and yelling—"Go to hell," "Scram" and "Get out of our country." Some in the crowd began pushing and shoving them, and The Beatles and their entourage started fearing for their lives.

"The Beatles, their road managers and myself were treated at the airport like animals," Epstein told Reuters. "We were punched, kicked, shoved and humiliated by strong-arm men, apparently present especially for our departure."

George told the AP, "We were terrified." Ringo Starr said they were "scared stiff."

"When they started on us at the airport, I was petrified," John said later. "I thought I was going to get hit so I headed for three nuns and two monks, thinking that might stop [the crowd]. As far as I know I was just pushed around, but I could have been kicked and not known it."[3]

---

2   *The Beatles Anthology*, p. 220
3   *The Beatles Anthology*, p. 220

When they were finally allowed to leave the terminal, "more than 500 persons ... jeered and booed as The Beatles walked to their plane," the AP reported. "Drummer Ringo Starr made a face at the crowd, and the insults hurled at them were intensified."

Once safely seated in the plane, they were still delayed from leaving. Epstein and two other managers were called outside. The Philippine government held the gate receipts from the two shows and authorities demanded the band pay taxes—on money they hadn't even received.

The Beatles were eventually allowed to take off, and they promptly vowed never to return. "If we go back, it will be with an H-bomb," John told the AP. "I won't even fly over the place."

Fame was taking a heavy toll. It was chasing them, it was trapping them, like a tossed boat caught between dark skies above and an endless ocean beneath— and no earthly destination seemed a safe harbor. Feeling beaten and exhausted from the Japan and Philippines experience, they traveled to India, hoping for rest and relaxation before heading home. Their main reason for stopping was so George could shop for a sitar. George also thought it would be a quiet place for them to lay over and recover. After all, it was a country in which they had no known following.

But upon arriving at Palam International Airport in New Delhi, an estimated 2,500 screaming Indian teenagers were on hand to greet them. "It was night-time," George says in *Anthology*, "and we were standing there waiting for our baggage, and then the biggest disappointment I had was a realization of the extent of the fame of The Beatles—because there were so many dark faces in the night behind a wire mesh fence, all shouting, 'Beatles! Beatles!' We got in the car and drove off, and they were all on little scooters [following us]. ... I thought, Oh, no! Foxes have holes and birds have nests, but Beatles have nowhere to lay their heads."

On July 30, the album *Revolver* hit No. 1 in the Billboard charts and stayed there for five weeks. As an artistic piece, it is arguably The Beatles at their very best, at their peak of creativity. The album was named the best ever in the book *Virgin All Time Top 1,000 Albums* (in 2000) and by the television music network VH1

The album cover for *Revolver* (left) is like a billboard advertisement for the method by which John Lennon would die 14 years later. The revolver that was used to kill Lennon is shown above in an official police photograph.

(2001), and was also voted as such by the readers of *Rolling Stone* (2002).

On the cover, the album's boldface title is like a billboard advertisement for the method by which John Lennon would die 14 years later. It's a point easily dismissed as coincidence, but there was plenty else amiss. Unusual messages began showing up in Beatles material, and each, in hindsight, seem profoundly prophetic. An explanation as to why the album was titled *Revolver* has never been given by The Beatles or anyone else involved in its production. The band had considered naming the record *Abracadabra*,[4] a word that in recent times has been associated mainly with entertainment and stage magicians, but for most of history was regarded as a mystical term used as an invocation to ward off disease and evil spirits.

One of the first songs John had written for the album was "Tomorrow Never Knows." In *Anthology*, he says the composition was inspired by his experimentation with marijuana and LSD, and by Timothy Leary's adaptation of the *Tibetan Book of the Dead*. John wanted to make a ghostly track with a spiritual sound, like monks chanting from high atop a hill. The final effect of the overall tone was created through the use of sound manipulations, including looped tapes and backward play. The song was considered

---

4   Miles, p. 269

revolutionary. Paul McCartney recalls in *Anthology*, "John just strumming on C rather earnestly—'Lay down [all thought, surrender to the void]. ....' And the words were all very deep and meaningful."

One of the stranger Lennon compositions to allude to death, "Tomorrow Never Knows" was originally titled "Mark 1." As an avid reader of the Bible, John would likely have been aware that the book of Mark contains nearly 80 mentions of demons and evil spirits (more than any other book), and also references instances of Jesus exorcising those demons. In Mark 5:1-20, Jesus was confronted by "a man with an evil spirit" while traveling to Gerasenes. The man calls for help and Jesus expels the demons from the victim's body. The possible significance of the song's original title cannot be overlooked, not only because of its connection with demons, but also because it matched the name of a young boy growing up in the 1960s in the suburbs of Atlanta, Ga.—Mark David Chapman, who would one day use a revolver to kill John. For that matter, the final title could be just as telling; by using "Tomorrow Never Knows," John may have been expressing uncertainty with his life and future:

> *Or play the game,*
> *Existence to the end*
> *Of the beginning ...*
> *Tomorrow never knows.*

Mark David Chapman would be the end of John's beginning.

During the recording sessions for *Revolver*, The Beatles worked on the track "Rain," which would eventually be released as a single. It contained recording-history's first use of reversed music and voices. While working on the song, John, high on marijuana, accidentally loaded the tapes backward, resulting in a sound that "transfixed" him. He called the inspiration "the gift of God—of Jah, actually, the god of marijuana. Jah gave me that one. The first backward tape on any record anywhere."[5] When "Rain" was released as a

---

5   *The Beatles Anthology*, p. 212

single, the U.K. advertisement used the "butcher cover" photograph to promote the record. It was an eerie combination: crumbled baby-doll bodies,
blood and raw meat, together with words and music played backward.

As is commonly known, backwardness (speaking or writing backward, the
use of reverse images, and so on) is often associated with demons and the occult, whether it be in fiction, literature or fringe religious practices. That fact
begs an important question: Is there a connection between the backwardness
in The Beatles' music and the backward practices of the occult? At least one
person close to the song seemed to think so—Ringo. He later commented
on his "Rain" drum work: "I think it's the best out of all the records I've ever
made. 'Rain' blows me away. It's out of left field. I know me and I know my
playing, and then there's 'Rain.'"[6] Additionally, in *Anthology* he says: "The
drumming on 'Rain' stands out for me because I feel as though that was
someone else playing—I was possessed."

Whether or not John was on a literal journey toward hell, in 1966 hell was
on a figurative journey toward him. Fame was about to get dramatically un-
comfortable.

On July 29, the U.S. teen magazine *Datebook* published Maureen Cleave's
five-month-old interview. On the front cover of the magazine, under the
blurb "The Ten Adults You Dig/Hate The Most," a small part of John's quote
was highlighted: "I don't know which will go first—rock 'n' roll or Christianity." Inside, the entire quote was repeated, including the assertion "we're more
popular than Jesus."

Though the original statement had drawn little attention in Britain, in
the U.S. (especially in the Bible Belt) the response was immediate and hostile. Just two days later, Tommy Charles and Doug Layton, disc jockeys for
WAQY radio in Birmingham, Ala., began a drive to ban The Beatles from the
airways. Additionally, they urged a boycott of all Beatles products and asked

---

6   Dowlding, p. 130

their listeners to send in their Beatles records, pictures and souvenirs for a huge "Beatle bonfire" set for August 19, the night the band was scheduled to play in nearby Memphis, Tenn. Charles called John's comment "absurd and sacrilegious" and said, "Something ought to be done to show them they cannot get away with this sort of thing."[7]

Within days, dozens of disc jockeys in the South joined the boycott and ban. E.Z. Jones of WBBB and Jack Starnes of WBAG in Alabama were among the first. And most of their listeners—youngsters included—agreed with their stance.[8] One Birmingham disc jockey, Rex Roach, said his station was receiving hundreds of Beatles records which they planned to pulverize in a municipal tree-grinding machine. He said, "After going through the 'Beat-

le-grinder' ... all that will be left of the records will be fine dust." He planned to present a box full of the remains to the band when they arrived in Memphis. In Birmingham, 14 collection points were set up for citizens to drop off Beatles paraphernalia, and traffic was brisk.[9] WTUF in Mobile, Ala., denounced John's statement as "not only deplorable but an outright sacrilegious affront to Almighty God."[10] In Lawton, Okla., KSWO disc jockey B.J. Williams called

Teenagers gather at a "Beatles Burning" in Waycross, Ga., where records, books and wigs were burned in a bonfire in response to John Lennon's comment that The Beatles were more popular than Jesus.

for their own Beatle bonfire, and cracked The Beatles' latest album while on the air. Only three of 75 listeners who called in to the show opposed him.[11]

7   United Press International, Aug. 4
8   *The Daily News Times*, Aug. 5, 1966
9   Reuters, Aug. 7, 1966
10   The Associated Press, Aug. 4, 1966
11   United Press International, by Peter J. Shaw, Aug. 5, 1966

WAKY in Louisville, Ky., aired ten seconds of silence every hour in lieu of playing a Beatles song, and asked listeners to use that time to pray.[12]

Though the backlash began in the Bible-Belt South, plenty of people in the North lent support. Donald Ballou, general manager of WSLB in Ogdensburg, N.Y., declared The Beatles "off my station."[13] In Fitchburg, Mass., WEIM suggested a Beatles ban and asked its listeners to phone in with their opinions; in eight hours, the station received 291 responses in favor of the boycott, and only 33 against.[14] Four Pennsylvania state senators introduced a resolution banning The Beatles from "all stages, radios, televisions and jukeboxes in the state."[15] Similarly, State Rep. Charles Iannello of Boston denounced The Beatles as "four creeps" and asked the Massachusetts House of Representatives to revoke the band's permit to perform at the city's Suffolk Downs Race Track on August 18.[16] In Milwaukee, WOKY Music Director King Zbornik declared that the station would not ban The Beatles until he saw John's comments for himself. "But I can believe he said it," Zbornid said. "I've been fed up with them ever since their latest album came out with [the 'butcher cover']. The way these guys have been acting lately is a real letdown for our kids. If they're going to take all of the American kids' money, at least they could be gentlemen about it."[17]

Religious leaders and churches also joined the protest. The Rev. Thurman H. Babbs, pastor of the New Haven Baptist Church in Ohio, threatened to expel any parishioners who attended the upcoming Beatles concert in Cleveland, and to ostracize any who dared to agree with John's opinion about Jesus' popularity. He declared, "It's high time Christians speak out on this atheistic remark."[18] Further south, the influential Florida-based Dutch Reformed Church asked congregations to destroy their children's Beatles records. "One feels shocked and disappointed about Lennon's statement," said one church leader. "We are grateful, however, for the wide reaction it has caused. I could never convince myself their music was a good example."[19]

---

12   *Oakland Tribune*, Aug. 5, 1966
13   The Associated Press, Aug. 4, 1966
14   United Press International, Aug. 4, 1966
15   *Bucks County Courier*, Aug. 9, 1966
16   The Associated Press, Aug. 12, 1966
17   United Press International, by Peter J. Shaw, Aug. 5, 1966
18   The Associated Press, Aug. 13, 1966
19   United Press International, Aug. 5, 1966

Newspapers also fortified the fray. A column in Delaware's *Daily Times* read, "The logical thing would be to burn The Beatles. Seriously. Ask The Beatles to come here and get an enormous mob and take them out and burn them up. Better still, ask John Lennon to volunteer to be burned. ... While he is being burned the other Beatles could sing 'Burn, Baby, Burn' or something equally appropriate. ... That way all offended religious people would be avenged, and there would still be three Beatles left to entertain us and shoot off their mouths."

In a widely syndicated editorial, influential preacher Dr. Norman Vincent Peale responded to John's "more popular" comment: "This rather curious statement came as a surprise since most intelligently informed people never thought of Jesus as making any effort to be popular. ... The brash remark of the cocky girl-haired young man may, of course, represent poor taste, but that aspect of the matter does not interest me at all. The thing that needs clearing up is, I believe, the implication that Jesus is in some kind of popularity contest with The Beatles. The disparity between the Master and these characters is almost complete for Jesus had nothing at all of material value. He never made a million dollars before shrieking teenagers or anyone else, for that matter. He lived the life of poverty and selflessness while the long-haired boys from Liverpool clean up the dough—and how! They are certainly far ahead of the simple man from Nazareth on that score."

The Beatle ban spread to other countries, too. In the Philippines, priests in the predominantly Catholic province of Laguna asked their congregations not to even listen to music by The Beatles; and Caloocan City, a suburb of Manila, passed a resolution banning the same.[20] In Johannesburg, the South African Broadcasting Corporation (SABC) announced a ban on all Beatles records pending clarification of John's comments. Piet Meyer, head of SABC, called for a full investigation and said the group's "arrogance" had grown unacceptable.[21] An Interior Ministry official said, "The Beatles will not be admitted to South Africa. A visit by them is regarded as being not in the best interests of the country."[22]

---

20   United Press International, Aug. 5, 1966
21   United Press International, Aug. 5, 1966
22   The Associated Press, Sept. 4, 1966

The world—inspirited by John's apparent blasphemy—was revolting against him. And he may have felt quite defenseless without the alliance that got him famous enough to be in that much trouble. The devil may have helped John gain fame, but he would not be shielding him from the God-fearing masses.

The Beatles responded to the controversy by, at first, not responding. A spokesman for the group told UPI, "To avoid further confusion and misinterpretation, neither John nor the other Beatles are commenting immediately."

In the meantime, Capitol Records quickly defended him. "[He was] quoted out of context and misconstrued," a label spokesman told UPI. "[His remarks were] conjectural on the topics of Christianity, rock 'n' roll and other institutions subject to change over the years. [John] only intended the broadest possible comparison between the rock 'n' roll movement and the institution of Christianity as it relates to trends of nonconformity among contemporary youth. He definitely intended no irreverence."

Epstein left a vacation and promptly flew to New York to assess the situation. While he didn't deny that John had made the controversial statement, he did assert that it had been misinterpreted. "What Lennon said and meant was that he was astonished that, in the last 50 years, the Church of England, and therefore Christ, had suffered a decline in interest," Epstein wrote in a press statement. "He did not mean to boast about The Beatles' fame." When asked by a UPI reporter if he believed The Beatles are more popular than Jesus, Epstein replied, "Of course not."

In England, Cleave, who had written the original article that contained John's quote, also publicly defended the musician. "I do not think for one moment that he intended to be flippant or irreverent," she told the AP. "He was simply observing that so weak was the state of Christianity that The Beatles were, to many people, better known. He was deploring rather than approving this."

All the protesting was occurring at a time when The Beatles were scheduled for a U.S. tour starting August 12. Meanwhile, in England, all four

Beatles were receiving death threats—so many that the menace had to be taken seriously. Epstein rarely turned to The Beatles with tangential issues, but thought it important to discuss the threats with John before the tour began. Interestingly, though, John had no reaction to his life supposedly being in danger; he was only concerned for Paul, George and Ringo.[23] Did John have no corporeal concern because he knew he would be safe from death for another 14 years?

On the morning of August 11, the band arrived at London airport for their flight to the U.S. According to UPI, on hand was a group of 500 supporters screaming that they would "start World War III" if Americans hurt their Beatles. One fan, 15-year-old Janet Turner, said, "I don't pray to Jesus, I pray to John." Other fans were chanting, "John not Jesus" and "The Yanks are mad."

Prior to The Beatles boarding the Pan Am flight, an airline spokesman placed Bibles at their seats as a "special gesture." The spokesman said, "As far as we are concerned The Beatles are in American territory as soon as they board the plane. ... I've never done any research on this, but it's the first time to my knowledge that this has been done. All our planes carry Bibles, of course, for passengers who ask for them."

When The Beatles arrived at Boston's Logan International Airport, 600 fans greeted them with the customary screams. Clearly they hadn't lost popularity among U.S. teens. Tight security kept the band away from crowds while they waited for a connecting flight to Chicago, where again a heavy police presence kept them isolated, even from the press.

But once settled in Chicago, The Beatles held a news conference. Media around the world covered the event, eager to hear the band's first public comments since the scandal commenced. For the first time in their careers, there were no teen-pop-idol questions, and the press immediately targeted John. He explained his thoughts about the quote that had caused so much trouble: "I wasn't saying whatever they're saying I was saying," he said. "I was just sort of deploring the attitude toward Christianity. It just seems to me to be shrinking, to be losing contact."

---

23   Coleman, p. 407

The Beatles held a second press conference the next day before their concert at the city's International Amphitheatre. Again reporters primarily questioned John, and he further explained the meaning behind his Jesus comment. "Originally I was pointing out that fact in reference to England—that we meant more to kids than Jesus did, or religion, at that time. I wasn't knocking it or putting it down, I was just saying it as a fact. ... [And] it is true, especially more for England than here. I'm not saying that we're better, or greater, or comparing us with Jesus Christ as a person or God as a thing or whatever it is, you know. I just said what I said and it was wrong, or was taken wrong. And now it's all this."

The reporters continued:

> **Q:** What do you think about that fact that you believe that it's true? What's your reaction to that truth?
> **John:** Well, my reaction is that I was deploring it, you know. I was pointing it out. I mean, if somebody like us says it, people sort of do take notice, you know—even church people are trying to be "with it" with pop groups and things. They're still doing it the wrong way, and I was just stating a fact as I saw it. And I wasn't trying to compare me or the group with Jesus or religion at all, but just only in that way—the way I'm trying to tell you.

> **Q:** Did you mean that The Beatles are more popular than Christ?
> **John:** When I was talking about it, it was very close and intimate with this person that I know who happens to be a reporter. And I was using expressions on things that I'd just read and derived about Christianity. Only, I was saying it in the simplest form that I know, which is the natural way I talk. But she took them, and people that know me took them, exactly as it was—because they know that's how I talk.

Q: Do you think you're being crucified?
John: No, I wouldn't say that at all.

Q: To what do you ascribe your immense popularity?
John, talking to Paul: You answer that one, don't you?
Paul: Really, if you want an honest answer, none of us know at all.

John's explanation and semi-apology seemed to be acceptable for most of the U.S.—even Birmingham's WAQY disc jockeys called for an end to the boycott they'd initiated. Controversy or not, teenage madness was on display during the two sold-out concerts in Chicago. The Beatles sang less than a dozen songs, acted like themselves, and produced the usual results: infectious screaming, unconstrained crying, collective swooning, periodic fainting. Approximately 180 policemen were on hand, but no spectators rushed the stage.[24]

Their next show was on August 14 at Cleveland Stadium, and it would not enjoy the same peaceful result. According to Ohio's *The Chronicle Telegram*, during the fourth song, "Day Tripper," an unidentified girl managed to climb the dividing fence and charge the stage. An estimated 3,000 people followed her lead, storming through police lines. As The Beatles finished the song, fans started climbing on stage, and one nearly pulled Ringo from behind his drum set. The police quickly escorted the band to the safety of a security trailer while they tried to restore order, causing a 30-minute delay in the concert. UPI reported that extra officers—dressed entirely in black—were then deployed to the stadium to form rings around the stage, and cars were parked on the field to create an additional barrier between crowd and band. The crowd was warned that the remainder of the show would be cancelled if anyone left their seat again. The fans complied until the last song, "Long Tall Sally," when they re-broke the barriers, rushed the stage and surrounded the trailer. Security hurried The Beatles into an awaiting black limousine which

---

24   *Oakland Tribune*, Aug. 13, 1966

took them out of the stadium. Speaking to an AP reporter, one police officer likened the chaos to recent race riots on Cleveland's East Side.

On August 19, The Beatles finally flew to Memphis, a town fundamentally divided about the boys from Liverpool. Ten days earlier the City Council had unanimously approved a resolution requesting that the band cancel their two scheduled performances, and local clergymen scheduled a Christian youth rally for the same time as the concerts. Still, each of the concerts sold out. During the performance, crowds were even rowdier than in Chicago—to the point of even more danger for The Beatles. During the second show, people in the balcony began throwing fruit, flashbulbs and other debris onto the stage. "There had been threats to shoot us, the [Ku Klux] Klan were burning Beatle records outside and a lot of the crew-cut kids were joining in with them," John says in *Anthology*. "Somebody let off a firecracker and every one of us … look at each other, because each though it was the other that had been shot."

Their Los Angeles experience was even worse. On August 28, The Beatles played at Dodger Stadium, which was heavily fortified in anticipation of trouble. Bob Thomas of the AP wrote, "[The] stadium looked somewhat like the Berlin border. Burly guards stood at the bottom and midway of each stairway leading to the field. Uniformed policemen with helmets and billy clubs lined the field, some of them communicating with walkie-talkies. Behind them were three rows of hurdles, then came a newly erected wire fence." At 9:33 p.m., Thomas writes, The Beatles emerged from the third-base dugout and 45,000 fans exploded with screams. A few of the crowd jumped from the stands to the field and raced toward the stage; they were quickly captured by police, handcuffed and led off the field, while onlookers booed. Later an officer was hit by an orange thrown from the upper deck, while onlookers cheered.

The show ended at 10 o'clock, and The Beatles jumped into their car, ready to make a quick exit from the ballpark. But fans were waiting. Tony Barrow, a Beatles public relations man who was with the band that night, recorded the experience in his book *John, Paul, George, Ringo and Me*. "By the time we were … ready to pull away, many hundreds if not thousands [of fans] had positioned themselves across our path," he writes. "[The driver] slammed his gears into reverse and we sped backwards across the field at breakneck speed. Panic-stricken fans flung themselves out of our way. I was amazed that we didn't smash into anyone. The trick failed to clear a path for our escape and the driver gave up. At high speed he headed for a dugout at the far side of the field and we hurriedly raced underground out of sight of the noisy hordes of fans." Barrow reports that they stayed secluded for two hours while police cleared the stadium, at which point they discovered their car had been "severely damaged and put out of action." They made three more attempts to leave using decoy limousines, and each try was thwarted. Eventually the police employed an armored car to bring The Beatles safely out.

The next night was their last of the tour. They played at San Francisco's Candlestick Park to 25,000 fans, a little more than half the stadium's capacity. Again, security precautions were severe. The stage was elevated above crowd level and enclosed by a 6-foot-high fence that was bordered by city policemen. An armored truck, its engine running, waited nearby to whisk The Beatles away after the show.

There was also something else special about this concert—something fateful and final—something that added to their on-stage actions. Before the show started, The Beatles put their own cameras on top of their amplifiers and set the shutter timers. "We stopped between tunes," George says in *Anthology*. "Ringo got down off the drums, and we stood facing the amplifiers with our back to the audience and took photographs. We knew."

The 1966 American tour (nicknamed by John "The Jesus Christ Tour"[25]) was over. It had stopped in 14 cities during the month of August. Nearly half a million people attended Beatles shows in Chicago, Cleveland, Detroit, Philadelphia, Toronto, Canada, Boston, Memphis, St. Louis, Seattle, New York City, San Francisco and Washington, D.C. For the band, touring had become a circus atmosphere, their concerts chaotic and tumultuous events.

---

25   Shotton, p. 129

Dealing with the Jesus-comment fallout at every stop made the crusade that much more grueling, driving the band to exhaustion.

After a press conference in September, a change was apparent. "The youth is gone from their faces. They seem ten years older. They are pale, seem overly tired, overly pressured. The fun may still be there for their fans but for them it looks as if the fun is gone," wrote John Larson of Ohio's *The Times Recorder*. "Their answers to newsmen's questions lack the old sparkle. They're not as free and witty as they used to be. Even the greetings to the smaller mobs of fans are less warm, less real. ... For The Beatles, it has been a hard day's night. And, it's beginning to show."

Now rich and famous, The Beatles no longer needed to accommodate the stress and trauma associated with traveling and performing for delirious fans. Their wealth and fame allowed them to spend more time in the studio away from chaotic public scenes—an effort that would lead them over new creative horizons, to writing and recording compositions that would change not only the music industry, but the very culture of the civilized world.

And so The Beatles flew home to England, their touring days over.

The Devil Is In The Details

Do we have to divide the fish and the loaves
for the multitudes again? Do we have to get crucified again?
Do we have to do the walking on water again
because a whole pile of dummies didn't see it the first time,
or didn't believe it when they saw it?
— John Lennon

One of the more intriguing storylines in rock history is the long, world-wide fascination with the rumor that Paul McCartney died in an automobile accident on November 9, 1966, and that The Beatles covertly replaced him with a look-alike and then concealed clues about the whole affair in their subsequent lyrics and album covers.

The origin of the rumor is a mystery. Its public outing, however, is not. According to the book *Art & Entertainment Fads* by Frank Hoffman and William Bailey, the story was first publicly spun in the September 23, 1969, issue of the University of Illinois' newspaper, *Northern Star*. A month later a Michigan college student phoned a disc jockey at Detroit's WKNR to ask about the legitimacy of the story, which sparked a two-hour on-air discussion of the clues. The topic was then picked up by WMCA radio in New

York, then quickly by other stations and newspapers across the U.S., and then around the world.

Soon after, Paul held a press conference during which he claimed, borrowing from Mark Twain, "Reports of my death are greatly exaggerated." Perhaps to provide further evidence, he still records and tours to this day.

The suspicion, however, was not without merit. The clues were there, and too numerous to be ignored. They just needed to be viewed through a different lens to create not a picture of a past conspiracy, but of a future tragedy. When examined as a possible prophecy, the clues appear to be quite clearly not about Paul, but about John Lennon.

By the end of 1966, success couldn't have gotten any greater for The Beatles. They were legends. Their fans numbered in the millions, their records sold by the millions. Not only had John become bigger than Elvis Presley, as he'd desired, but he'd also become, in his own words, "more popular than Jesus." If he had made a deal with the devil, then the devil had certainly fulfilled his end of the bargain.

For John, that would surely have been a harsh reality. His journey from nearly abandoning his aspirations to being history's most popular musician lasted only six years. There were 14 years left for him to enjoy that success, for him to fret about its cost, for him to reflect and regret and maybe try to atone. Those years would not be quiet, but rather riddled with reminders and clues of what was to come.

An early example—possibly the first clue to John's fate—can be seen on the cover of the album *A Collection of Beatles Oldies*, released on December 10, 1966. It's curious, if not downright suspicious, that the word "oldies" would be chosen for the title, considering that a number of the tracks, such as "Eleanor Rigby" and "Yellow Submarine," had been released that same year. One need not look far, however, for an explanation. John's full birth name was John Winston Lennon; but upon his second marriage in 1969, it would change to John Ono Lennon, making his initials JOL. The album cover features a man sitting center. His crossed right leg, with only slight imagination, can be seen as the letter "J," and it rests aside the word "OLDIES" written on the face of a bass drum. All the letters are the same color, making their relation to one another

The cover of the album *A Collection of Beatles Oldies* spells out that "JOL (John Ono Lennon) DIES."

clear. Together, they spell "JOLDIES"—or, "JOL DIES." This message puts to rest the question as to whether or not John Lennon and The Beatles were knowingly planting death clues themselves. This craftily constructed prophecy appeared 16 months before John legally changed his middle name to Ono.

It would not be the last time a drum head would impart a message. *A Collection of Beatles Oldies* was only the beginning of what would be a colossal collection of clues, and it was but one note compared to the symphony of messages that awaited in The Beatles' next album. No record in their catalog would contain more uncanny communications than *Sgt. Pepper's Lonely Hearts Club Band.*

The Beatles had passed a turning point in their careers. They were no longer the "Fab Four" of the early 1960s, a clean-cut, well-groomed package of formally dressed lads. The cover of *Sgt. Pepper* reflected that change, depicting The Beatles in their old image alongside The Beatles dressed in brightly colored military outfits, sporting mustaches and spectacles.

Does the *Sgt. Pepper* album cover reveal the scene of John Lennon's funeral? Was this scene predicted in the first lyrics of the album's title song, "It was 20 years ago today"? Was that when the devil first struck his deal with Lennon and "taught the band to play"?

They are surrounded by a large crowd of historic figures, famous and inspirational people, including Marilyn Monroe, Karl

Marx, Edgar Allan Poe, Albert Einstein, Lawrence of Arabia, Mae West and Sonny Liston. Also prominent is the image of Aleister Crowley, one of the century's most famous occultists who referred to himself as "The Great Beast."[1] *Time* magazine wrote that the crowd appears as if "gathered around a grave." In front is a mound of dark dirt, looking much like the site of a fresh burial. Atop the "grave" grow blood-red hyacinths arranged to spell "Beatles." At the bottom stands the Hindu goddess Kali, who was supposed to have destroyed demons,[2] but who is also reputed to be "held responsible for smallpox, plague, cholera and other pestilences that beset mankind, and for the high fevers that rage before death."[3] The flower arrangement also contains a number "3" and a guitar with just three strings—both supposedly indicating that only a trio of Beatles remained. The title track is also the first on the album, and begins with the lyric "It was 20 years ago today." When looked at together, one could deduce that this album cover was predicting the future: a funeral scene, a freshly dug gave, and all were gathered to pay respects to the fallen Beatle, 20 years after he made his deal with the devil and became a star almost overnight.

The very next lyric on the record offers another clue. The entire first line of the song is, "It was 20 years ago today, Sgt. Pepper taught the band to play." If the 20 years is indeed a reference to the length of the pact between John and Satan, then this may be an admission that the devil (in the semblance of Sgt. Pepper) helped The Beatles learn to write the extraordinary songs that brought their wealth and fame.

Still more clues appear on the flip side of the album. The back cover is bright red, possibly signifying the great loss of blood that would preclude death and burial, or perhaps the red glow of fire in hell. The original back (since redesigned) is also covered with lyrics to the album's songs (incidentally, the first time in recording history this was done). The Beatles stand at the bottom, and George Harrison is pointing toward the words for "She's Leaving Home"—specifically at the line "Wednesday morning at five o'clock as the day begins." In later years, conspiracy theorists would proclaim this to be one of the clues

---

1   Crowley, p. 15
2   Harding, p. 64
3   Cavendish, p. 1,464

that Paul had died (in a car accident at 5 a.m. on a Wednesday). It does appear to be a clue, albeit misinterpreted. If one follows the line of George's point even further, the eye comes to the lyrics of his song "Within You Without You":

We were talking—about the space between
    us all
And the people—who hide themselves
    behind a wall of illusion.
Never glimpse the truth—then it's far. too
    late—when they pass away.

We were talking—about the love that's gone
    so cold
And the people who gain the world and lose
    their soul—
They don't know—they can't see—are you
    one of them?

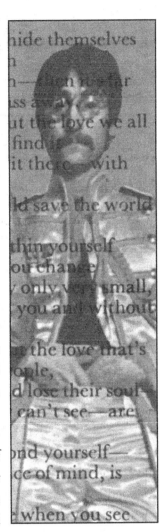

The words "lose their soul" are printed directly across John's beltline, perfectly centered. In the accompanying photo, John is facing forward and Paul backward. Was he turning his back on John and what he knew of the fatal pact?

Years after the album's release, another mysterious message was discovered on the cover of the *Sgt. Pepper* album. In his book *The Walrus was Paul*, R. Gary Patterson describes how John was influenced by the writer Lewis Carroll and his unique wordplay. Reading Carroll's novel *Through the Looking Glass* inspired Patterson to use a small, flat mirror to search for messages in

The words "lose their soul" are printed directly across the beltline of John Lennon on the back cover of *Sgt. Pepper.*

the reflections of the *Sgt. Pepper* cover. He was particularly interested in the photograph's bass drum, as its design was credited to Joe Ephgrave—con-

ceivably a fictitious moniker coined by combining the words "epitaph" and "grave," which would further make the drum a fitting headstone for a deceased Beatle. "The bass-drum skin looked, at first, innocent enough with the album title psychedelically etched across its surface," Patterson writes. "The two phrases 'Sgt. Pepper's' and 'Club Band' were angled to the top and bottom of the drumhead and in similar design. The phrase 'Lonely Hearts' was of a different design

Was the mirrored message on the *Sgt. Pepper* drum—"I ONE IX HE DIE"—a message from the devil boasting, "I won, nine he die"? John would die December 9 in Liverpool time.

and was placed in the center and in psychedelic print. The different pattern appeared awkward. Why wasn't the same lettering used for the complete album title?

"By holding the mirror perpendicular to the cover and in the dead center of 'Lonely Hearts' a hidden message appeared between the glass and cover. The message read: 'I One IX He Die.'"

Patterson's interpretation, published in 1996, was intended as another clue in the Paul-is-Dead myth: that the cryptic drum-face message translated to the date Paul had supposedly perished. "I One" meant "11," "IX" was the Roman numeral 9, and together they supported that Paul succumbed on 11/9 (November 9).

But Paul is not the one who died—John is. The message points much more perfectly to that instead. "I ONE IX HE DIE" can easily be read as a proclamation from the devil, boasting "I won, nine he die." John would, 13 years after the album's release, die on December 8, but at 10:50 p.m.—which was actually December *ninth* in Liverpool, where his fame, and presumably his pact, began. Furthermore, "HE DIE" appears within the word "hearts." When John was shot, the bullets entered through his back on the left side of his chest, destroying major blood vessels leading to his heart.

Sgt. Pepper was released on June 1, and was quickly hailed as brilliant creativity that would likely change the course of popular music. *The Times* of London praised it as "a decisive moment in the history of Western civilization," and it would go on to become the first rock record to win a Grammy for Album of the Year.

Brian Epstein had been somewhat involved with the 129-day production of *Sgt. Pepper*, but was not as busy with the band as in the past; most of his job had revolved around the logistics of concerts and other public appearances, and The Beatles never intended to follow this album—or any other again—with a tour.

Moreover, Epstein hadn't been the same since The Beatles stopped performing. Rather, he'd gone into a deep depression. "What will I do if they stop touring?" Epstein asked Peter Brown. "What will be left for me?"[4]

In *The Beatles Anthology*, Ringo Starr describes the effect that the band's new direction had on their manager: "Brian's role with us had changed because he wasn't booking us around the world any more. We were working in the studio, we'd make a record and the record would come out. What was there left for him to do? Book the studio—one phone call."

Toward the end of summer, The Beatles were in the small town of Bangor in North Wales to meet with Eastern mystic and spiritual mentor Maharishi Mahesh Yogi. During the trip, they received unwelcome news.

---

4   Brown, p. 192

"There was a phone call," George recounts in *Anthology*. "I don't know who took it. I think it might have been John. Blood drained from his face: 'Brian's dead.'

"There was very little we knew other than that he'd been found dead."

Epstein, The Beatles' manager throughout their sudden rise and reign at the top of the music world, had succumbed to an overdose of sleeping pills. Authorities recorded the death as accidental.

The timing of Epstein's death is notable. Once John's rise to the top was complete, his manager was gone. That fact is feasibly coincidence, but could also be attributed to the idea that when one deals with the devil, sometimes an intermediary is used either to arrange the pact or to carry out the deeds that fulfill it. In fact, Maximilian Rudwin writes that historically Jews have acted as such intermediaries for Christians, not because the former have any sort of sinister leanings, but simply because "the zealot in one religion prefers a zealot to a liberal even in an opposing religion." Epstein—who, incidentally, was Jewish—undeniably piloted John's path to fame. And once that path reached its destination, once an intermediary was longer needed, Epstein disappeared.

The manager's death was the beginning of the end of The Beatles. "After Brian died, we collapsed," John said later. "Paul took over and supposedly led us. But what is leading us when we went round in circles? We broke up then. That was the disintegration."[5]

In the late fall of 1967, The Beatles began working on a film and accompanying album titled *Magical Mystery Tour*. For the album cover, they once again dressed in costume: One stands center in a black walrus outfit, while the other three appear behind as a white rabbit, parrot and hippopotamus. One of the Paul-is-Dead clues claimed that a walrus is a symbol of death in certain Scandinavian countries, that Paul is the Beatle dressed as a walrus, and therefore he must be dead. However, the truth is that Paul was not dressed as the walrus. John was, which is clear in the film. Either way, the identity of the tusked one is irrelevant; the idea that a walrus is symbolic of death

---

in any folklore, Scandi-
navian or otherwise, isn't
supported anywhere—
it's urban legend within
urban legend.

However, while the
walrus as costume may
not carry the weight of a
clue, the walrus as lyric
certainly does. "I am the
Walrus" was the first song
John wrote after Epstein
died, at a time when John
may have first truly com-
prehend his pending fate.

First, it should be noted
that John admitted that

The walrus, rumored to be a symbol of death in some
Scandinavian countries, is featured on the cover of the
Magical Mystery Tour album. The film that accompanies
the album clearly shows that John Lennon is the walrus.

the imagery in the song is at least partly nonsense and that he thought it
"ridiculous" that people have tried so hard to analyze its lyrics.[6] However, if
the devil or a demon or any other supernatural force wanted to plant clues
in a work of art, the artist certainly wouldn't need be to be aware. The words
and phrases within "Walrus" definitely provoke some interesting questions.
They're full of symbols and images of death and confusion, including "pigs
from a gun," "choking smokers," "pigs in a sty," "yellow matter custard drip-
ping from a dead dog's eye," "pornographic priestess" and John hauntingly
screaming, "I'm crying, I'm crying."

The song begins with a simple keyboard vamp that sounds like the oscil-
lation of a police or ambulance siren, soon laid over by an ominous chord.
If there is any question as to who the walrus is, John answers it in the first
three words: "I am he." The second stanza contains the lyric "stupid bloody
Tuesday"—offering the day of John's eventual death (in Liverpool time) and a
description of the scene (John would lose a tremendous amount of blood).

---

6   *The Beatles Anthology*, p. 273

The last stanza mentions Edgar Allan Poe (whose picture, incidentally, was included on the *Sgt. Pepper* cover), a tormented writer who was obsessed with death, violence and trag-edy, best known for his tales of the macabre. Poe is recognized as the father of the modern mystery genre, and trickery and deception are common themes in his work. His 1832 short story "Bon-Bon"—originally titled "The Bargain Lost"—is about a man who tries to sell his soul to the devil, and his 1841 story "Never Bet the Devil Your Head" is a satirical parable with an evident ending. Walt Whit-man defined Poe as a writer with "an incorrigible propensity toward nocturnal themes, a de-moniac undertone behind every page." Lennon and Poe both died at 40 years old.

Album artwork from *Magical Mystery Tour* shows The Beatles as wizards (top) and shows John the walrus at the piano (bottom).

The most consistent sym-bol in "I am the Walrus" is the eggman—it's the only thing mentioned more often than the walrus. What does it represent? The egg is one of the most ancient symbols in humankind, having a rich tradition in religion and culture. Almost uni-versally, the egg represents transition from non-existence to life—generation, birth and rebirth. The egg is also symbolic in occult lore, and, according to *The Encyclopedia of Magickal Ingredients*, is used by witches in myriad spells.

The song builds toward the end with an orchestration of violins, cellos and horns, and then some befitting old-English recitation. In *Anthology*, John says, "There was some live BBC radio. They were reciting Shakespeare or something and I just fed whatever lines were on the radio right into the song." The lines, it turns out, are from Williams Shakespeare's *King Lear*, and just happen to speak prophetically of death:

> **Oswald:** Slave, thou hast slain me. Villain, take my purse.
> If ever thou wilt thrive, bury my body,
> And give the letters which thou find'st about me
> To Edmund Earl of Gloucester. Seek him out
> Upon the British party. O, untimely death!
> **Edgar:** I know thee well—a serviceable villain,
> As duteous to the vices of thy mistress
> As badness would desire.
> **Gloucester:** What, is he dead?
> **Edgar:** Sit you down, Father, rest you.

What do these lines mean to John's prophecy? In 1980, Mark David Chapman would shoot John ("Slave thou hast slain me") to, he said, steal his fame ("Villain, take my purse").[7] Though he would be cremated, John had said he wanted his body buried after death ("bury my body").[8]

The final tell of the song may be in the tale that prompted its title: the Carroll poem "The Walrus and the Carpenter." In his life, John, the walrus, may surely have deceived his fans by achieving success through dubious means. This very idea is reflected in lines 91 to 94 of the poem:

> "It seems a shame," the Walrus said,
> "To play them such a trick.
> After we've brought them out so far,
> and made them trot so quick!"

---

7   *The Daily Herald*, Aug. 25, 1981
8   Goldman, p. 690

In a photo as it appears exactly with the *Magical Mystery Tour* album, John stands in front of a store, next to a window in which a sign reads, "Best way to go is by M&D C." Was this a message that the best way to go—or die—was by MDC, or Mark David Chapman?

Is that how John was feeling as he finally fathomed the reality of his success?

Even more clues are provided in photos that accompany the *Magical Mystery Tour* album, which portray The Beatles as magicians and witches. The words on the inside of the liner notes begin, "AWAY IN THE SKY, beyond the clouds, live 4 or 5 Magicians. By casting WONDERFUL SPELLS they turn the Most Ordinary Coach Trip into a MAGICAL MYSTERY TOUR."

But the biggest clue, the most predominant predictor of the future, lies in a picture of John alone. He's standing in front of a store, next to a window in which a sign reads, "Best way to go is by M&D C." It was a fatal message: MDC—Mark David Chapman.

"I think by 1968, we were all a bit exhausted, spiritually," Paul says in *Anthology*. "I think generally there was a feel of, 'Yeah, it's great to be famous, it's great to be rich, but what's it all for?'"

John battled personal troubles, too. He impregnated artist Yoko Ono, whom he had met the previous fall, while still married to Cynthia Powell. He hadn't tried to hide his relationship with Yoko, which hurt his public image and, of course, his marriage. He and Powell traded accusations of infidelity, argued about money, then filed for divorce.[9]

Led by George's example, The Beatles headed to India for a weeks-long meditation retreat with Maharishi Yogi. Not all of them shared George's dedication, but they did all gain from the experience. "Regardless of what I was supposed to be doing, I did write some of my best songs while I was there," John says in *Anthology*. "The experience was worth it if only for the songs that came out." The work from the trip included the compositions "Yer Blues," "Sexy Sadie" and "Dear Prudence"—all of which would appear on their next album, the eponymous *The Beatles*, commonly referred to as "The White Album." The new release was the first for Apple Records, the new label founded by the band that year. With a new album, of course, came new clues.

One clue was placed deliberately, in the song "Glass Onion," though only as a red herring. The Paul-is-Dead theorists claimed that a glass onion represented a coffin with a transparent lid. In the song, John sings:

> *To see how the other half lives,*
> *looking through a glass onion.*

Then in the next stanza he adds:

> *Here's another clue for you all:*
> *The walrus was Paul.*

But John claimed he wasn't offering insight into Beatles conspiracies. Instead, he said he was mocking them. "That line was a joke," he told *Playboy* in 1980. But how much of a joke was it, really? John specifically writes of offering "another clue"—almost two years before talk of the Paul-is-Dead theory was first documented. Had John begun to recognize the inadvertent clues to his own death, and was he now proactively trying to divert attention from himself and toward Paul?

---

9   Coleman, p. 444

Regardless of John's intentions with that song, a later track on the album is one of the most comprehensive collection of clues in all The Beatles' work: The track "Revolution 9" is alone a significant study in the analysis of auditory symbols. A Lennon composition—or perhaps "construction" is the better term—"Revolution 9" is the epitome of the backwardness and hidden messages prevalent in Beatles material. Recorded in May and June of 1968, it remained one of John's favorite and most autobiographical recordings. The other Beatles tried to exclude it from the White Album, but John prevailed. Mystery has surrounded its content ever since.

John described the making of "Revolution 9" to *Playboy*: "The slow version of 'Revolution' on the album went on and on and on, and I took the fade-out part … and just layered all this stuff over it. It has the basic rhythm of the original 'Revolution' going on with some 20 [tape] loops we put on, things from the archives of EMI. We were cutting up classical music and making different size loops, and then I got an engineer tape on which some test engineer was saying, 'number nine, number nine, number nine.' All those different bits of sound and noises are all compiled. There were some ten machines with people holding pencils on the loops—some only inches long and some a yard long. I fed them all in and mixed them live. I did a few mixes until I got one I liked."

The 8-minute, 15-second track took 18 takes to record—it was a mission of dedication. "I spent more time on 'Revolution 9 than I did on half the other songs I ever wrote," John said.[10]

"With so many overlapping sounds, it is almost impossible to identify all the individual noises and spoken comments," writes Steve Turner. "Mark Lewisohn, who studied the original four-track recording, divided these into: a choir; backwards violins; a backwards symphony; an orchestral overdub from 'A Day In The Life'; banging glasses; applause; opera; backwards mellotron; humming; spoken phrases by John and George, and a cassette tape of Yoko and John screaming the word 'right' from 'Revolution.'"

Words spoken in the song foretell—with eerie accuracy—what would happen on the night of December 8, 1980:

---

10   Cross, p. 429

0:02—"*number nine, number nine, number nine*"—When played backward, phonetically "number nine" can be heard as "turn me on, dead man." The reversed clip maintains a most fiendish tonal quality, almost from the beyond, the voice again and again commanding, "Turn me on dead man, turn me on dead man, turn me on dead man." Additionally, the final note from the song "A Day in the Life" is dubbed numerous times throughout. In that song John sings, "I'd love to turn you on," which is undeniably similar to "turn me on, dead man."

1:14—"*Humpty Dumpty*"—John whispers the name of this nursery-rhyme character. The egg is a reoccurring theme in John's compositions. In "I am the Walrus" he sings, "I am the eggman, they are the eggman," and in the movie *Magical Mystery Tour*, multiple references are made to an egg. The poem "Humpty Dumpty" is simple and meaningful in its parallel to John's story: "Humpty Dumpty sat on a wall. Humpty Dumpty had a great fall. All the kings horses and all the kings men couldn't put Humpty together again."

1:20—"*intended to pay/die for it*"—John says, "He intended to pay for it." When he says "pay," the word "die" is overlaid. He intended to pay/die for it. A fitting confession to a contract with the devil?

1:51—"*Who was to know! Who was to know?*"—George, first exclaiming, then asking, sounding dejected.

2:15—"*on the third night … unfortunately*"—Chapman arrived in New York City on Saturday, December 6, 1980. On Monday, the third night of his visit, he shot and killed John—unfortunately.

3:40—"*With the situation … they are standing still*"—Chapman positioned himself quietly at the front gate of the Dakota apartments, waiting for John to return from a night in the recording studio. It was a critical and problematic situation. Chapman stood still as John passed him, and then turned and fired at John's back. Officer Pete Cullen, one of the first two policeman to arrive at the apartment building, said he was surprised by the lack of movement at the scene: The doorman, a building handyman and the killer were "all standing as if frozen."[11]

3:58—"*Who can tell what he was saying? His voice was low and his eye was high*"—After being shot, John choked and gurgled.[12] Throughout the song John can be heard making gurgling, choking and moaning sounds that are haunting, threatening, alarming, strange, painful, unpleasant and horrifying. After being shot, police carried John's body to the back seat of their squad car and drove him to the hospital. The officers said they could hear him mumbling and moaning.[13]

4:13—"*he's on fire*"—This maybe suggests that John, upon death, had reached an unfavorable afterlife destination—the fires of hell.

4:14—"*his glasses were saved*"—Yoko saved the eyeglasses John wore that night. Within a month of his death, Yoko released the album *Season of Glass*, featuring the bloodied spectacles on the cover.

4:56—"*we'd better go to see a surgeon*"—Upon arrival at the hospital, attending physician Dr. Stephan Lynn and his team

---

11   The Associated Press, Dec. 3, 2005
12   Goldman, p. 686
13   United Press International, Dec. 9, 1980

surveyed John's internal injuries and determined there was no way to save him.[14]

5:31—"*my broken chair, my wings are broken and so is my hair*"—A declaration that all is not right.

5:49—Sounds of gunfire.

6:08—"*only to find the night watchman unaware of his presence in the building*"—José Perdomo, the night watchman in the sentry box at the Dakota, allowed Chapman to sit on the curb and wait for John to return home. While Perdomo was aware of Chapman, he was clearly unaware of the sinister force within.

6:32—"*must have hit between his shoulder blades*"—Chapman fired five shots from his revolver. Four of the bullets entered John's back, between his shoulders.

6:44—"*Take this brother, may it serve you well*," with the sounds of a cash-register drawer opening and a door slamming shut—As mentioned earlier, Chapman said he murdered John to capture his fame. One police detective commented, "It's an old rule. You become as famous as the guy you kill. This kind of killing brings names closer together than marriage."[15]

7:05—"*good fishes again in the kettle*"—"Kettle of fish" is an old Scottish term that means "a fine mess."[16] The *Mirriam-Webster Unabridged Dictionary* defines it as "a bad state of affairs" or "a thing to be … reckoned with." Also, as noted earlier, John once told Pete Best that he would do anything to achieve success: "It

---

14   *The New York Times*, Dec. 8, 2005
15   The Associated Press, Dec. 19, 1980
16   Claiborne, p. 143

might cause some heartache, but once I'm up there it'll be a different kettle of fish."

7:45—"*you become naked*"—On the afternoon of December 8, John and Yoko posed for *Rolling Stone* photographer Annie Leibovitz. One of the photos from the shoot was used for the cover of the magazine's Lennon commemorative issue of January 22, 1981; the photo was of John naked, cuddling with Yoko. Some might say the image has an uncanny look and a feel of occult and Satanic influence.

7:47—The chant of a crowd at a sporting event, "*hold that line, hold that line*" and "*block that kick, block that kick*"—John's death was announced to the U.S. during *Monday Night Football* by Howard Cosell, who was working the game as commentator. Cosell: "An unspeakable tragedy confirmed to us by ABC News in New York City: John Lennon, outside of his apartment building on the West Side of New York City, the most famous perhaps of all of the Beatles, shot ... in the back, rushed to Roosevelt Hospital, dead on arrival."

John may or may not have been aware of what the track was foretelling, but he did know the song was a prediction of *something*. He says in *Anthology*, "'Revolution 9' was an unconscious picture of what I actually think will happen when it happens, just like a drawing of a revolution."

The track also has a direct connection with the occult. Charles Manson, who led his cult followers in a series of murders in the 1960s, claimed that he received secret messages through Beatles songs that were written specifically to direct his actions. The composition that impacted him the most was "Revolution 9." In the book *Helter Skelter*, author Vincent Bugliosi, the lead prosecutor in the case against the Mason family, writes that Charles believed The Beatles were prophets who were looking for Jesus Christ, and that he was the Christ they were looking for. "Almost every song in [the White Album] had a hidden meaning, which Manson interpreted for his followers," Bugliosi writes. This was especially the case with "Revolution 9." In one part of the song, John screams "right." Manson misheard the word as "rise," and interpreted it as an incitement to the black community to rise against the white middle class. "Rise" became one of Manson's key phrases found painted in blood at one of his murder scenes.

Bugliosi also notes that Manson believed "Revolution 9" was a reference to the Bible's Revelation 9, which reads: "And in those days shall men seek death, and shall not find it; and shall desire to die, and death shall flee from them. And the shapes of the locusts were like unto horses prepared unto battle; and on their heads were as it were crowns like gold, and their faces were as the faces of men. And they had hair as the hair of women, and their teeth were as the teeth of lions. And they had breastplates, as it were breastplates of iron; and the sound of their wings was as the sound of chariots of many horses running to battle. And they had tails like unto scorpions, and there were stings in their tails: and their power was to hurt men five months. And they had a king over them, which is the angel of the bottomless pit."

This Bible reference could be read as describing The Beatles ("locusts" are insects, as are beetles), with their guitars ("breastplates of iron"), their music chords ("tails like unto scorpions") and the loud, amplified music ("the sound of chariots of many horses running to battle"). For their time, The Beatles had unusually long hair ("the hair of women"), and they had power. Considering the centuries that have passed since Revelation was written, its parity to The Beatles is disturbingly apparent.

One last note to be explored about this all-important song involves a particular of John's behavior during the time he was recording it. Many who enter into a contract with the devil become not only a victim of the power of the pact, but they also become deluded by it. In the same way Faust boasted of performing more miracles than Jesus, at one point John believed he *was* Jesus and wanted to announce as much to the world. Pete Shotton writes that had the following encounter with John during the early recording sessions of "Revolution 9":

"One night, after a few joints, a bit of LSD, we were sitting around at Kenwood playing tapes when John suddenly said: 'Pete, I think I'm Jesus Christ.' 'You what?' I said. 'I'm Jesus Christ. I'm back again.' 'Oh yeah,' I said, 'what are you going to do about it?' 'I've got to tell the world who I am.' 'They'll kill you.' 'That can't be helped,' said John. 'How old was Jesus when they killed him?' 'I reckon about 32.' 'Then I've got at least four years to go,' said John. 'First thing tomorrow morning, we'll go into Apple and tell the others.'"

The next morning Shotton contacted the label to arrange an emergency board meeting. All four Beatles turned up, plus Neil Aspinall (once The Beatles' roadie, later Apple's managing director) and Derek Taylor (their press officer).

"Right," said John, sitting behind his desk. "I've something very important to tell you all. I am ... Jesus Christ. I have come back again. This is my thing."

The Beatles looked rather stunned, but said nothing. "It was totally surreal," Shotton writes, wrapping up the story. "But nobody cross-examined him. No plans were made to announce the Messiah's arrival. There was a bit of muttering, then silence, till somebody suggested the meeting was adjourned for lunch. In the restaurant over lunch, a man came up to John and said: 'Really nice to meet you, how are you?' 'Actually,' said John, 'I'm Jesus Christ.' 'Oh, really,' said the man. 'Well, I liked your last record.'"

The final year of the 1960s would also be the final for The Beatles. They had two albums left in them, *Let it Be* and *Abbey Road*. Though recorded in 1969 in that order, the latter was released first.

The cover of *Abbey Road* was yet more fodder for the Paul-is-Dead theorists. The Beatles are pictured walking across Abbey Road, a scene rumored to represent a funeral or death procession. John, dressed in white, supposedly symbolized religion, or God or Jesus himself; Ringo, wearing a tuxedo, was the church or minister, or a pallbearer; shoeless Paul was death; and George wearing blue jeans was a gravedigger or undertaker. One of the cars in the background was said to be a black hearse waiting for the transport of the body and coffin for burial.

 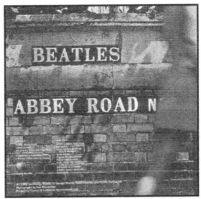

The album cover for *Abbey Road* (left) was interpreted as a funeral procession, while the back cover shows a skull and a sign for the "three" Beatles. The album's first song, "Come Together," begins with John Lennon singing "Shoot me."

The background of the back cover is a picture of a brick and concrete wall. The upper line of the brickwork separates the word "Beatles" at the top from "Abbey Road" at the bottom. At the upper left, eight dots rest inexplicably on the wall; they look like they could be marks left by bullets, in the same way that Chapman's bullets would strike a building years later.[17] Connected, the holes form a "3" in front of "Beatles." Near the center, a crack in the concrete runs through the "s" in "Beatles"—suggesting a flaw in the band. At the right is the blurry image of a female wearing a blue dress, walking out of the scene. Her identity has never been revealed. She could be, or could be representative of, Satan (devil with a blue dress on?). Behind her, a shadow appears on the wall; outlined and viewed sideways, it appears to be a skull. The lines of the contours of her back form an "x" which, under the skull, form the image of crossbones. Together, they are the nearly universal symbol of death and danger—possibly another reminder to John of the perdition that awaited him.

The first song on *Abbey Road* is John's composition "Come Together." In retrospect, the song seems highly biographical and prophetic, containing references to death and the occult, starting with the title. One event where people "come together" is a funeral; and at the end of each verse John gravely sings, "Come together right now over me." The lyrics also mention: "juju," an object or charm that has supernatural power; "mojo," voodoo or

---

17   United Press International, Dec. 9, 1980

black powers of supernatural origin; and "holy roller," a typically disparaging term for a member of a religious denomination in which spiritual fervor is expressed by shouts and violent body movements. The line "he got early warning" could reveal that John was aware of his allotted time, a clue that he had dappled in magic. He also sings "one and one and one is three," perhaps another indication that only three Beatles would remain after the earlier warning was carried out.

But the most profound clue of "Come Together" is a partially obscured invitation in the intro. The song begins with a distinctive and famous bass lick accompanied by a whispered lyric that has been half hidden to listeners ever since. The Beatles' sound engineer for the song, Geoff Emerick, explains: "On the finished record you can really only hear the word 'shoot.' The bass guitar note falls where the 'me' is."[18] John isn't singing just "shoot"—he's singing "shoot me." Throughout the song he repeats again and again, "shoot me ... shoot me ... shoot me," in an inviting and most challenging manner.

The *Let it Be* cover was simple: each Beatle in a separate candid portrait, arranged in a square on a black background. Black, a color often associated with death and mourning, was an appropriate backdrop for their final album. The color is also suggestive of dark undercurrents, evil characteristics or forces that are wicked or dishonorable—black deeds, a black sinister heart, or a future that looks black, offering little or no hope.

The song "Let it Be" was widely interpreted to be about Virgin Mary, the mother of Jesus. However, Paul really wrote the song for his mother, Mary, who died when he was 14.[19] But if there was a subliminal force in Paul's writing, the lyrics could have been advice for John's spiritual predicament:

> *When I find myself in times of trouble*
> *Mother Mary comes to me*
> *Speaking words of wisdom, "Let it be."*
> *And in my hour of darkness*

---

18   Dowlding, p. 277
19   Turner, p. 180

She is standing right in front of me
Speaking words of wisdom, "Let it be."

If John had heard those lyrics in the religious regard, he might have noticed a way out of his pact. For those who deal with the devil, there is a way to save their soul: constant prayer to the better half of the spiritual world. According to Rudwin, in the medieval era, prayer to the Virgin Mary was considered by the church to be "the surest way … to avoid paying the penalty" of losing one's soul to Satan.

Also on their last released album was a song that John had penned much earlier, before The Beatles were even The Beatles: "One After 909." He wrote the song in the late 1950s, and the band first recorded it in the studio in March 1963.[20] Then the song inexplicably went in the archives until resurrected and re-recorded for release on *Let it Be*.

If songs containing messages of John's destiny were ranked by content, "One After 909" surely would be at the top. Not only is the analyzed prediction accurate, but it's uncanny that he wrote the song so early in his career. It seems that from the very beginning the timeline and the events leading to John's death were described with the utmost of accuracy and detail in this one composition. If John had fully understood the meaning of what he was writing, then he must have known he was likely powerless to change his destiny. However, if he didn't understand, then the words could only have been channeled through him from a presumably supernatural source. Either way, the song's message is far too accurate to be a coincidence.

Many things are at play in the lyrics, a complex web of related components. First, John had already predicted in "I am the Walrus" that he would die on a "stupid bloody Tuesday" (again, in Liverpool time). It was the only composition in which he ever referenced a day of the week, making the line that much more surely relevant as a clue. Second, the importance of the number nine in John's life cannot be downplayed. Even he recognized it: "I was born on 9th October. I lived at 9 Newcastle Road. Nine seems to be my num-

---

20   Miles, p. 536

ber so I've stuck with it, and it's the highest number in the universe; after that you go back to one. It's just a number that follows me around."[21] He saw the number not only in his past, but even in his future: In the book *We All Shine On*, Paul Du Noyer writes, "[John] once predicted that he would die on the ninth day of the month."

John believed in numerology, the study of numbers to reveal hidden truths about one's existence. Author Robert Rosen had access to John's diaries and wrote a posthumous biography about the last five years of the former Beatle's life, titled *Nowhere Man: The Final Days of John Lennon*. Rosen writes, "Lennon dove headlong into numerology. It was just what he needed. Numerology could quickly be applied to any situation to get a preliminary reading on the future. … John and Yoko were unable to walk out of the house without finding mystical significance in every license plate, address, and street sign. They would not so much as dial a telephone number without first consulting their bible, *Cheiro's Book of Numbers*, which could have been subtitled 'Numerology Made Easy.'"

One of the fundamentals of numerology is that any series of numbers, particulary dates, can be decoded by a method called "digit summing." The process involves adding the string of numbers together, often multiple times, until the result is a single digit.[22] For example, John would die in 1980, which reduces to the number 9 ($1 + 9 + 8 + 0 = 18$, then $1 + 8 = 9$).

To see how this concept is important to "One After 909," one need only look at a calendar of 1980. Again, in "I am the Walrus," John had already provided the day he would die: Tuesday. And in 1980, only twice would a ninth day of the month fall on a Tuesday: in September and December. The American shorthand for September 9 is "9/09." But that's not the Tuesday when John died, December 9 is; he died on the *second* Tuesday-the-ninth of the year, the "one *after* 9/09." In one simple lyric, John provided his moment of death down to the month and day.

A continued examination of the lyrics reveals even more:

> *My baby says she's trav'ling on the one after 909.*
> *I said, 'Move over honey, I'm traveling on that line.'*

21   *The Beatles Anthology*, p. 307
22   Drayer, p. 20

Clearly John is traveling, or leaving, on "the one after 9/09," Tuesday, December 9, 1980.

> *I said mover once,* [to Tuesday, September 9]
> *Move over twice,* [to Tuesday, December 9]
> *Come on baby, don't be cold as ice.*

Dead bodies are often morbidly described as being "cold as ice."

> *I said I'm trav'ling on the one after 909.*
> *I begged her not to go and I begged her on my bended knees,*
> *You're only fooling around, you're only fooling around with me.*

John may have begged to be spared from death, spared from hell. When he realized he would not be saved, he may have tried to cope with his fate by choosing to believe he was only being fooled around with.

> *Pick up my bag, run to the station,*
> *Railman says you've got the wrong location.*
> *Pick up my bag, run right home,*
> *Then I find I've got the number wrong.*

If John knew when he would die, then he probably wanted to be home, in a presumptively safe place, to try to avoid his fate—just as Pope Sylvester II sidestepped Jerusalem in an effort to avoid his. But like the devil fooled Sylvester, maybe he fooled John, too. John was to die on the ninth based on the time zone of Liverpool, not New York—he was using the calendar of the "wrong location," and thus he also "got the number (the date) wrong."

We do know that John tried to get home before the clocks of New York struck midnight. On the evening of the assassination, he had been recording at a studio in Manhattan. He declined an offer to dine out afterward because he wanted to hurry back to the Dakota—and he succeeded, stepping out of his limousine at nearly 11 o'clock.[23] "Bag" (or "old bag") is slang for a female significant other, such as a girlfriend or wife, and John did run home with Yoko. Had he realized the date trick and rushed back to the Dakota to perceived safety?

By the beginning of 1970, The Beatles were effectively finished. All that was left as a group was to tidy the details for *Let it Be*, and to argue.

John moved on with his music career, recording as a solo artist and with Yoko. One of his hallmark achievements, the *Imagine* album, was released in Britain on September 9, 1971. The date was the ninth day of the ninth month in a nine year (1 + 9 + 7 + 1 = 18; 1 + 8 = 9). The label on the record features a close-up portrait of John looking pensive. The sleeve contains the song credits printed in nine spiraling circles. When viewed together, they form a clear picture of John at the center of a target, with the record's center-hole resting right between his eyes. Meanwhile, the album's cover shows a foggy image of a man who had sadly chosen the wrong path.

Was the sleeve of John Lennon's album *Imagine* a symbol for a target with Lennon at the center? The center-hole rests right between his eyes.

The song "Imagine"—John's signature post-Beatles work—is a utopian, new-age mantra. He said it was an "anti-religious, anti-nationalistic, anti-conventional, anti-capitalistic song, but because it's sugar-coated, it's accepted."[24] The lyrics are about a fictional, impractical place: John imagines a world without heaven or hell, no religion, no borders, countries or war. His desire for no heaven or hell is disparaging to Christianity, for it requires an abandonment of God and the holy scripture. And for a man who may have been feeling apprehensive about the future consequences of what he had done, imaging no heaven and

---

23   *Newsweek*, Dec. 22, 1980
24   *Rolling Stone*, Dec. 5, 2005

no hell may have given him comfort. He may have been trying to rationalize his predicament—it may perhaps even be viewed as a form of denial.

The *Imagine* album was in part a response to Paul's album *Ram*, released earlier that year. John thought two of Paul's songs were directed at him: "Too Many People," with the lyric "You took your lucky break and broke it in two"; and "Back Seat of My Car," which alleged, "Oh, we believe that we can't be wrong."

John's response to Paul was rapid and direct with his songs "How Do You Sleep" and "Crippled Inside." The former contained the lines "Those freaks was right when they said you was dead" and "The only thing you done was yesterday, and since you're gone, you're just another day."

John told *Playboy* in 1980, "You know, I wasn't really feeling that vicious at the time. But I was using my resentment toward Paul to create a song, let's put it that way. He saw that it pointedly refers to him, and people kept hounding him about it. But, you know, there were a few digs on his album before mine. He's so obscure other people didn't notice them, but I heard them. I thought, Well, I'm not obscure, I just get right down to the nitty-gritty. So he'd done it his way and I did it mine."

Aside from lyrics, Paul's album may have included more symbolic messages directed at John. The most obvious at the time of release was the back cover, which included a picture of two beetles copulating—almost surely representing Paul's bitterness about the breakup of The Beatles and the subsequent legal battle between them. But the strongest message appears on the album's front cover: a photograph of Paul holding a ram by the horns. The ram

Was Paul McCartney taunting John Lennon by reminding him of his deadly ties and his debt to the devil by naming his album *Ram*, known as a symbol for Satan? Did John believe the image was about him, and did he retaliate with the photo that accompanied *Imagine* of him mimicking Paul's ram pose by holding a pig by the ears?

has deep roots in Satanism, so deep that the devil is often depicted as a ram, or as a man with the head of a ram. Was Paul taunting John, reminding him of his deadly ties and his debt to the devil? John possibly believed the image was about him, because he retaliated in the photos that accompanied *Imagine*—one depicts him mimicking Paul's ram pose, but instead holding a pig by the ears.

Satanists deny the link, but many people believe a ram's horns are the basis of the "corna"—a salute made by forming a fist and then raising the index finger and pinky—which became commonplace in heavy metal concerts of the 1980s. Like any hand gesture, the corna's meaning varies between cultures; but in the 60s, it was widely viewed in the English-speaking world as being Satanic. The same is true of the "O.K." hand sign, formed by creating a circle with the thumb and index finger and

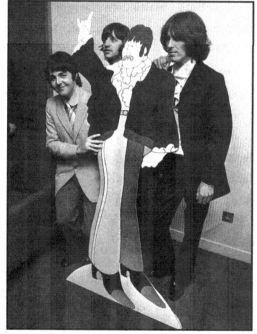

In the publicity photo for The Beatles' album *Yellow Submarine*, John Lennon is shown displaying what is interpreted as a satanic corna sign, symbolizing the devil's horns. Lennon's gesture is also seen on the album's cover and in cartoon cardboard cutouts used to promote the movie that accompanied the album.

leaving the last three fingers pointing straight up; if the circle is viewed as the bottom of a "6," then the three fingers become the top of three sixes, creating a "666" (defined as "the number of the beast" in modern translations of the Bible). On the jacket of the *Yellow Submarine* album, John makes the corna sign in the cover illustration and in a promotional photo. In the latter, Paul is seen making the "666" sign.

As John's solo career continued, even more clues ensued. In October 1974, Apple released another of his albums, *Walls and Bridges*. The cover was a picture John had drawn as a boy, featuring a soccer player wearing a jersey with the number nine. The second single from the album was "#9 Dream," which peaked at No. 9 on the *Billboard* charts. The song's hypnotic and spellbinding chorus, "ah, böwakawa, poussé poussé," is comprised of nine syllables. John had originally titled the composition "So Long" (a phrase commonly used to bid farewell), but changed it precisely because of his interest in numerology and his belief of the personal importance of the number.[25] The song offers yet another set of lyrics uncanny in its premonition of John's life and fate:

> *So long ago,*
> *Was it in a dream, was it just a dream?*

The passage of time often blurs the distinction between dreams and reality. In those lines, John is admitting that he is unable to tell if what he sees happening in six years is perhaps believable reality or only a bad dream.

> *I know, yes I know,*
> *Seemed so real, it seemed so very real to me.*

In the opening stanza, John appears to have realized, possibly in a dream, exactly what will transpire the night he is to die.

> *Took a walk down the street*

---

25   Noyer, p. 90

John was walking from the street to his apartment when he was fired upon.

Thru the heat whispered trees.

This imagery is ambiguous. Could it be referring to the devil whispering through the trees of Central Park across the street from the Dakota, coming for John?

I thought I could hear, hear, hear, hear
Somebody call out my name

Many news reports claimed that as John stepped toward the building, Chapman called out, "Mr. Lennon!"—which Chapman has denied ever doing.[26]

As it started to rain.

It started to rain bullets.

Two spirits dancing so strange.

Could the two spirits dancing be John and the devil?

Dream, dream away.
Magic in the air, was magic in the air?

He is describing an almost dreamy, mystical state. Magic, of the occult variety, was in the midst of happening. This line is also reminiscent of a lyric from Ricky Nelson's song "Garden Party"—"Yoko brought the walrus, there was magic in the air."

I believe, yes I believe.

---

26   Jones, p. 45

Any confusion about if the song—or the dream—was being truly prophetic, is now gone. John knows what will happen.

More I cannot say, what more can I say?

More he cannot say, indeed. He sounds reluctant to divulge any more guarded information than is necessary. Considering the price he paid for his "more popular than Jesus" remark, he had to wonder: What might be the impact of a published song, containing even more controversial material, played again and again throughout the millennia? Further, what more *could* he conceivably say? The events of his last moments on this earth were laid down here for all to see.

On the river of sound,
Thru the mirror go round and round.

He is possibly referencing the round drum head on the *Sgt. Pepper* cover that, when viewed with a mirror, prophesizes his death.

I thought I could feel, feel, feel, feel
Music touching my soul.

It was music that brought him to this place where he would finally settle his debt with the most valued of possessions, his soul.

Something warm, sudden cold,

The wounds from hot bullets would result in warm blood streaming from his body, followed by the sudden cold of death.

The spirit dance was unfolding.

Again he returns to singing of the spirit dance, as if describing a ritual, obsessing over the most haunting part of the dream as it comes to fruition.

And lest one think John regarded his destiny lightly, he provides clear evidence to the contrary. In another song on *Walls and Bridges*, "Scared," John expresses fear of what is to come:

I'm scared, I'm scared, I'm scared.
I'm scared, so scared.
I'm scared, I'm scared, I'm scared
As the years roll away
And the price that I paid
And the straws slip away.

You don't have to suffer,
It is what it is.
No bell, book or candle
Can get you out of this, oh no! …

I'm scared, I'm scared, I'm scared
Every day of my life.
I just manage to survive,
I just wanna stay alive.
You don't have to worry.
In heaven or hell,
Just dance to the music.
You do it so well, well, well!

Hatred and jealousy, gonna be the death of me,
I guess I knew it right from the start.
Sing out about love and peace,
Don't wanna see the red raw meat,
The green-eyed goddamn straight from the heart.

I'm tired, I'm tired, I'm tired
Of being so alone,
No place to call my own,
Like a rollin' stone.

These lyrics show a singer who is frightened of the future. John borrows from William Shakespeare in saying, "No bell, book or candle can get you out of this," essentially saying that no church, no lighted candle, no prayer, can help him escape the doom he freely chose.

Number Nine

The world of nature exists within a larger pattern of cycles,
such as day and night and the passing of the seasons.
The seasons do not push one another; neither do clouds
race the wind across the sky; all things happen in good time;
everything has a time to rise, and a time to fall.
Whatever rises, falls, and whatever falls shall rise again;
that is the principle of cycles.
— Dan Millman, *The Life You Were Born to Live*

"**N**umerology is the study of a cosmic code that uses numbers as symbols," writes Ruth A. Drayer in her book *Numerology: The Power in Numbers*. "[It] lifts a curtain, which allows people to see deeply into their life talents, abilities and purpose."

Toward the end of his life, John was using numerology and astrology on a daily basis, allowing it to influence his decisions of travel, vacation, public appearances, business purchases, meetings and hiring decisions.[1] He was preoccupied with the occult and the metaphysical science of consciousness and spiritualism. Pete Shotton writes that the last time they saw each other, John "spoke almost exclusively about mysticism and the occult."

---

1   Rosen, p. 63; Seaman, p. 36

Numerology is based on the idea that a soul chooses when to come into the world and what name it will use once here. By studying these details, we can reverse-engineer our life, which allows us to understand our past and to predict our future. But it doesn't trump free will. "While numerology actually lays out a blueprint of each of our lives," Drayer writes, "there is no way to predict completely the choices we will make."

Many forms of numerology exist, and they date back as much as 11,000 years in myriad cultures. In fact, Drayer notes, the use of numerology was open and commonplace until around the dawn of the 18th century, when advances in science pushed it underground. Hans Decoz and Tom Monte write in their book *Numerology* that "The Chinese, Japanese, Greeks, Hebrews, Eqyptians, Phoenecians, early Christians, Mayans and Incans all employed number systems to gain a deeper understanding of themselves and the universe." In Western culture, the type of numerology most used is the Pythagorean system, developed before 500 B.C. by the Greek mathematician and philosopher Pythagorean.

According to Pythagorean numerology, much in nature can be revealed by numbers, dates, words and names, which can all be reduced through digit summing to the single numbers of one through nine, or the "basic numbers." (The exceptions are the numbers 11 and 22, "master numbers," which are not always reduced. Other master numbers also exist, but they are rarely encountered, according to Shirley Blackwell Lawrence, author of *The Secret Science of Numerology*.) The basic numbers can also reveal general qualities about a person, in the same way that astrology signs are thought to do. The interpretations are general and wide-ranging, but may offer some further insight about John. He said the number nine held a special significance and meaning throughout his life,[2] and the data supports his belief. "A nine … is a sign that the person is born to give loving service in a profession or in the arts," Lawrence writes. She also notes, "Turn the nine upside down and you have the six: the voice that must be heard."

---

2   Coleman, p. 68

Additionally, the number nine holds powerful significance in mythology and paranormal history and has long been associated with the devil and evil. Henry Cornelius Agrippa, author of *Three Books of Occult Philosophy*, writes that the number has "a great and occult mystery." Anne Christie, author of *Simply Numerology*, notes that some Hebrew scholars have actually referred to nine as "the devil's number." And W. Wynn Westcott, in his book *Numbers: Their Occult Power and Mystic Virtues*, describes the suspected powers of nine: "The ancients had a fear of the number nine and its multiples, especially 81; they thought them of evil presage, indicating change and fragility. At the ninth hour Jesus the Savior died. Nine is also 'the earth under evil influences.'"

Additionally, Satanists delight in reversing, mirroring and inverting symbols, letters and numbers (such as an inverted cross or backward language, or how an inverted star becomes the pentagram, and so on); and, as previously noted, six and nine become each other when mirrored and inverted.

John's life, viewed through the application of numerology, was rife with the numbers nine and six.

The Number Nine in John's Life

John Lennon was born on October 9.

His time of birth was at 6:30 p.m. (6 + 3 + 0 = 9).

He was born at General Hospital 126 (1 + 2 + 6 = 9).

He lived with his mother Julia in Liverpool on 9 Newcastle Road.

The registration number of the car that killed Julia was LKF 630 (6 + 3 = 9), driven by a police officer with badge number 126 (1 + 2 + 6 = 9).

As a student in Liverpool, John took—and failed—the General Certificate of Education exam nine times.

John's son Sean was also born on October 9.

In New York City, John lived on 72nd Street (7 + 2 = 9) in apartment 72 (7 + 2 = 9) of the nine-floor Dakota building, which was constructed in 1881 (1 + 8 + 8 + 1 = 18; 1 + 8 = 9).

The night in 1960 when The Beatles first drew a crazed, enthusiastic crowd in Litherland, England—the night the "magic" began—was December 27 (7 + 2 = 9).

Beatles manager Brian Epstein first went to see the band at the Cavern Club in Liverpool on November 9.

Epstein died in 1967 on August 27 (2 + 7 = 9).

The house John bought for his Aunt Mimi was on 126 Panorama Road (1 + 2 + 6 = 9).

In 1980, Mark David Chapman purchased a .38 caliber revolver at a Hawaii gun shop (from a salesman named Robin Ono, no less) on October 27 (2 + 7 = 9).

During Chapman's first trip to New York City in the fall of 1980, he stayed at the Olcott Hotel at 27 (2 + 7 = 9) West 72nd (7 + 2 = 9) Street.

During Chapman's second trip to New York, he stayed at the YMCA on West 63rd (6 + 3 = 9) Street. He checked in on December 6 (inverted 9).

On December 7, Chapman moved to the Sheraton Center and stayed on floor 27 (2 + 7 = 9).

Chapman referred to the killing of John Lennon as a continuation of J.D. Salinger's novel *The Catcher in the Rye*. During his murder trial, Chapman said that killing John was the new Chapter 27 (2 + 7 = 9) of the book.[3] (The actual number of chapters is 26. Mark felt he was taking the book to its conclusion.)

After John was shot, he was rushed to Roosevelt Hospital on 9th Avenue in Manhattan (nine letters) where he was pronounced dead at 11:07 p.m. (1 + 1 + 7 = 9).

The Number Nine in John's Music

One of the first songs John wrote was titled "One After 909."

His early band, Quarry Men, has nine letters.

The song "I am the Walrus" was influenced by the Lewis Carroll poem "The Walrus and the Carpenter." The poem is 108 (1 + 0 + 8 = 9) lines long, composed in 18 stanzas (1 + 8 = 9).

The song "Revolution 9" on the White Album contains a looped recording of an engineer repeating the phrase "number nine."

The song following "Revolution 9" is titled "Good Night" (nine letters).

The title of John's solo album *Mind Games* contains nine letters, as does the title of his album *Rock and Roll*.

In 1974, John released *Walls and Bridges*, his ninth solo album, in September (the ninth month of the year).

The cover of the *Walls and Bridges* album features a picture John drew as a child. It depicts a soccer player with "9" on his jersey.

Walls and Bridges included the song "#9 Dream," which peaked at No. 9 in the U.S. charts. The song's hypnotic chorus, "ah, böwakawa, poussé poussé," has nine syllables.

Other Number Nines

"Liverpool" has nine letters.

Paul McCartney's last name contains nine letters.

Dialing the name "John Lennon" on a telephone key pad produces the number string "5646536666," which contains six sixes (inverted nines).

In 1969, John officially changed his middle name from Winston to Ono. "John Ono Lennon" on the phone keypad is "5646666536666"—nine sixes.

John once warned that he would die on the ninth day of a month.[4] He also mentioned that one of his most famous lyrics— "All we are saying is give peace a chance"—contains nine words, and he noted that his name (John Ono Lennon) combined with his wife's (Yoko Ono Lennon) produces nine O's.[5]

Chapman's wife Gloria did not want to publicly talk to anyone about her husband's murder of John Lennon, but her uncertainty was dispelled when she said she received a sign from God telling her it would be all right to speak: One night while attending mass, Gloria was paging through the Bible. She randomly stopped in the book Acts of the Apostles. As she read the passage, the pastor simultaneously asked his congregation to open their Bibles to the very same verse she was reading. In that verse, the lord speaks to Paul in a night vision; God says, "Do not be afraid any longer, but go on speaking and do not be silent; for I am with you." Gloria said she had previously prayed to God to give her a sign, to let her know it would be O.K. to speak. She had been looking specifically for the word "speak" as a sign from God.[6] That verse read during mass? Acts 18:9 (1 + 8 = 9).

---

4   Noyer, p. 91
5   Coleman, p. 682
6   *People*, March 2, 1987

John's Nine-Year Cycle

Another important concept in numerology is that of the nine-year cycle. In his book *The Life You Were Born to Live*, Dan Millman explains: "Circles and spirals of time loop back on themselves in endlessly repeating patterns and rhythms. The universe expands and contracts in the rhythm of a cosmic breath that takes billions of years. ... We often experience smaller cycles, not often noticed in the business of everyday life—repeating patterns of energy that appear, disappear, and reappear, cycling upward in time, rising even higher as we learn the lessons of life, rising toward our destinies."

The philosophy of the nine-year cycle is that differently numbered years will yield different sorts of challenges and experiences. It was a nine year, 1980, when John died. Working backward in three nine-year cycles brings us to:

> In 1962, Ringo Starr officially joins the band, consummating The Beatles as a group—the "Fab Four."

> The Beatles sign their first record contract on May 9, 1962. Here the number nine appears twice, once in the date and again in the year $(1 + 9 + 6 + 2 = 9)$.

> They start recording for Parlophone on June 6, 1962. The month and day are sixes (inverted nines), in a nine year.

Moving ahead nine years:

> In 1971, John releases what is considered to be his signature solo album, *Imagine*. It is released on September 9, 1971—the ninth day of the ninth month of a nine year $(1 + 9 + 7 + 1 = 18; 1 + 8 = 9)$.

Moving ahead another nine years:

> John is shot and killed on December 8, 1980—but in his hometown of Liverpool, the date is already December 9. The year 1980 is a nine year $(1 + 9 + 8 + 0 = 18; 1 + 8 = 9)$.

Along the same lines of hidden meanings and messages is the art of the anagram—rearranging the letters of a word or phrase to reveal other words and phrases that were otherwise concealed. According to *The Encyclopedia Britannica*, anagrams are thought to be a Hebrew creation: Kabbalist Jews "were fond of [anagrams], asserting that 'secret mysteries are woven in the numbers of letters.'"

"The Beatles" was a curious choice of name for a band, especially because it's spelled wrong. In 1961, John wistfully explained to *Mersey Beat* where he got the idea: "It came in a vision—a man appeared on a flaming pie and said unto them, 'From this day on you are Beatles with an A.'"

So really, why "The Beatles"? Was it divine inspiration or Satanic intervention? Perhaps it's the latter; an anagram for "The Beatles" is "seal the bet"—as in a bet, or a deal, with the devil. An anagram for "man on a flaming pie" is "pagan flame minion"—was the man in John's vision a servant of Satan?

As mentioned earlier, history and legend suggest that sometimes when a person makes a Satanic pact, the devil delivers his end of the bargain via a human facilitator. "The devil could act on a matter distinct from himself through a direct act of local motion or by using an intermediary," writes Andrew Cooper Fix in *Fallen Angels*. "With God's permission the devil could make bodily material obey him, and in this way he often worked through other creatures." Is it possible that John received his payment through an intermediary? The Beatles' manager, Brian Epstein, is the man responsible for creating the steps the band took to climb to the top. He peddled their material, secured them a record contract and organized their tours and public appearances. Once The Beatles achieved ultimate fame and legendary status, once John admitted they were "more popular than Jesus," once the devil had won the bet—Epstein died.

Anagrams of "Brian Epstein" include: reap bet in sin; nines bet pair; Bea nine spirt ("bea," as in "Beatles with an A"); insane bet RIP ("rest in peace"). The common element of these anagrams is "bet." Entering into a pact with the devil is purely evil, for it revolves around a bet; it is gambling with hell.

As many of his biographies attest, much of the aforementioned was no secret to John. He was not only aware of what numerology reflected and predicted about his life, but he also believed those revelations to be true.

In 1981, journalist Robert Rosen was allowed to study the diaries John wrote in his last five years. As noted earlier, Rosen used that knowledge as the basis of his biography *Nowhere Man: The Final Days of John Lennon*. One of the common themes in the book is what numerology divulged about John's day-to-day affairs and his pending fate.

"[John saw] there was a lot of good in [his] numbers," Rosen writes. "The problem was that the bad seemed to overwhelm it; the numbers were stacked against him. There were too many indications of catastrophe, violence, premature death. But John didn't need *The Book of Numbers* to tell him that. He had felt it in his soul for as long as he could remember. Psychics could sense it when they looked at him. The numbers only confirmed it."

The Devil Went Down To Georgia

He who is tempted and tormented by the devil,
though he retain nothing else of his own, still retains his will;
but he who is possessed by him, who is become a demoniac,
belongs to him utterly and completely, body and soul.
— Arturo Graf, *The Story of the Devil*

Those who knew Mark David Chapman, the man who murdered John Lennon, were bewildered by his violent act. Most found it difficult to believe the person they had come to know would be capable of harming anyone, let alone a musician he had once idolized.

His friend and former boss David Moore told the *Chicago Sun-Times*, "I was watching the *Today* show on television … and when they said police were holding Mark David Chapman, I almost fell out of my chair. When we worked together resettling the Indochinese refugees for the YMCA, he was just a fantastic kid."

His mother Diane recalled to *People* magazine, "I pretty well know there was nothing that drastic in our lives that would cause anything like that. As far as I can see, we were pretty normal."

Chapman's father, David, did not want to speak to reporters about his son. His only statements came from a brief phone conversation with a writer for *The New York Times*. He described Mark as "industrious, cheerful and likable" in his younger days. "It's just like a different person than I used to know," he said. "I just think the buildup came in the last three years. Something must have happened to him after high school."

A former girlfriend told the television news program *Frontline*, "[I try to] separate the Mark that I knew from what really happened. And it's not—it wasn't Mark. It just wasn't. ... He couldn't have been in his right mind when he did it. There's just no way."

Is it possible that Mark David Chapman really wasn't himself on December 8, 1980? Is it possible that the violent tendencies that murdered John Lennon were being channeled through Chapman from another source? Is it possible that Chapman was acting under supernatural influence, perhaps demonic possession? Was Chapman the tool the devil was using to collect John's soul? Such scenarios are more common than most people realize, if we are to believe Father Gabriele Amorth. And we should consider believing him—he's the chief exorcist for the Roman Catholic Diocese of Rome, a man who London's *Sunday Telegraph* called "the most senior and respected member of his calling." Amorth admits that only about ten percent of the cases presented to him are actually legitimate possessions. In fact, he suggests that before people call him, they first consult a doctor. Still, he says, that ten percent are very real, if difficult to discern. "It is not easy [to identify a possession]," he told the *Telegraph* in 2000. "The devil does not like to be seen, so there are people who are possessed who manage to conceal it."

Authorities on such matters, Amorth included, categorize possessions based on different symptoms and degrees. But—borrowing from Kurt Koch's *Occult Bondage and Deliverance*, a guide to treating such cases—the general signs that a person is under demonic influence include despair, depression, defiance, spite, restlessness, involuntary body movements, thoughts of suicide, "lack of peace," "the feeling of being persecuted," "fits of fury" and violent behavior. Another trait is oscillating philosophies toward God and how to live one's life. "One day [the possessed] is moody, unresponsive and stubborn, the next day he starts to call on God for mercy," Koch writes. "One moment he promises never to drink again, or to break with all his other bad habits, yet in next to no time he has gone back on his word." Also, he writes, "the secret desire to murder someone is a persistent thought in the mind of many."

Additionally, the victim is often unaware that any of these traits and behaviors are related to being possessed. The demon avoids the spotlight, preferring to act as puppet master. "Desiring to remain anonymous, [the devil] injects his thoughts into those he has taken captive," Koch writes. "At a later date they may fail to understand how they were capable of such utterances and actions."

Though their work remains mostly unnoticed, exorcists of all religions tend to be busy people. As of 2008, Amorth alone had performed over 70,000 exorcisms.[1] Their workload consists of cases very familiar in history, religion and lore. "One can still find people whose condition bears a striking resemblance to the recorded cases of possession in the Bible," Koch writes, "and for which there is no other really satisfactory psychiatric or psychological explanation."

Almost all the aforementioned symptoms appeared in Chapman's life.

Mark David Chapman was born on May 10, 1955. He was still quite young when his mother Diane noticed the first signs of something amiss: As a baby, Chapman would rock and shake severely. "We had to take the casters off his crib, because he would rock it right across the room," she told *People* magazine after the murder. "And it carried on to quite an old age—maybe 12—just rocking back and forth all the time." Their doctor said not to worry.

Another sign appeared when Chapman was 12. That's when he first told his mother about the kingdom of Little People. "A lot of times with Mark I just thought he was kidding, because he did have a good sense of humor," she told *People*. "I said, 'What do they do?' And he said they sat along the wall. I guess he said he talked to them. I didn't pay that much attention."

---

1   Catholic News Agency, June 6, 2008

The Little People did more than indulge in polite conversation. They revered Chapman as their ruler. In *Let Me Take You Down*, biographer Jack Jones writes that Chapman doesn't remember when the Little People first appeared. "It was as though they had always been there, since the day he was born," Jones writes. "The Little People had remained invisible until a morning when he had awakened to see them coming and going from their homes, offices, and shopping centers inside his bedroom walls. At first, he thought it odd that no one else could see them."

Chapman's first rock 'n' roll album was *Meet the Beatles*, a gift from his father. He would listen to the record for hours a day. One morning, he modified four plastic army-man toys, cutting off their guns and replac-

ing them with plastic guitars and a set of drums he made from cardboard. He constructed a tiny stage and placed the plastic Beatles in front of an audience of Little People, and he imagined beaming a radio broadcast into their homes.[2] He read the back of the album cover and learned that The Beatles hailed from the seaside port city of Liverpool, and that a wild enthusiasm followed wherever they traveled. He read about a 16-year-old girl who spent four nights outside a ticket booth to hold her place in line, about a group of frantic school-girls battling police to gain access

Mark David Chapman as photographed by the New York City Police Department in the early morning of December 9, 1980.

to a sold-out show, about playing for Princess Margaret and the Queen Mother, about coming to America to be on Ed Sullivan's television show.

---

2   Jones, p. 98

He studied the photos. "He put his face close against the album, scrutinizing each of the four musicians," Jones writes. "He had trouble identifying John Lennon, whose picture looked oriental. On the front of the album, however, Lennon's face seemed full and round. His lips were a thin, straight line, not as defined or interesting, Mark decided, as the faces of the other three Beatles. After studying Lennon's features for a long time, he decided that he didn't especially like the face. He didn't know why."

Chapman sat and continued listening to the "concert" and began violently rocking, smashing his head into the couch so hard that the vibration caused the record needle to skip. As the song "Little Child" began to play, Chapman summoned the Little People and began singing to them, changing the lyrics to "Little People, won't you play with me? … Little People, you must stay with me." He then thought of a fight his parents had the night before, and how his father had hit his mother, and how it hadn't been the first time that had happened. A rage grew within, and he redirected it toward the invisible society around him. He started pushing imaginary buttons and making noises of explosions and gunfire; the Little People began screaming as their homes and buildings collapsed and fell, and others plunged from windows, and others were crushed and trapped by debris. Chapman surveyed the damaged and said, "That's what happens when I get angry."[3]

But Chapman was absolved. "They all kinda worshiped me, you know. It was like I could do no wrong," he told *People*. "The People would still forgive me for that, and you know, everything got back to normal."

If this imaginary world was a training ground built by demons, it was working perfectly. In this kingdom, Chapman found acceptance. He was allowed indefinite authority to commit violent crimes that he willfully executed. Reality became blurred. The make-believe acts of brutality could poison his judgment, making it difficult to choose a righteous path in real life. He could become desensitized toward the actual violence he would one day commit.

As he entered adolescence, Chapman left his world of Little People and immersed himself in the late-1960s culture of music and drugs. In 1969, at

---

3   Jones, p. 101

age 14, he began sniffing glue, smoking marijuana, snorting cocaine and tripping on LSD. He hated his parents, skipped school, grew his hair long, ran
away to Florida, came home and spent a night in jail for a narcotics violation.[4]
His life had changed, as had his personality. He was on a bad path, but for
the first time he felt like he belonged to a crowd—albeit a drug crowd.[5] His
new heroes, the musicians of the hippie era, sang of world peace, love and
freedom, and Chapman enthusiastically followed their call. And not unlike
millions of other kids looking for direction and answers during that time,
Chapman turned to The Beatles—not the "yeah-yeah-yeah" Beatles, but the
new, psychedelic, introspective Beatles that had been leading the music and
culture revolution he had become part of.

LSD has different effects on different people. For Chapman, it awakened a
dark internal disturbance. During one overnight drug party, he said he felt the
presence of an evil "spiritual force" residing within him. "We were all tripping
and I had this real scary experience," he says in *Let Me Take You Down*. "I was
standing up in the room and everybody else was lying out, passed out on the
bed. And I remember there was a knife. There was a knife in the room. Something in me, while I was tripping … was trying to urge me to pick up this knife
and stab it into these guys, into my friends." He resisted the compulsion, but it
was finally clear that a battle between good and evil was raging inside him.

In the summer of 1971, Chapman broke from the drug scene—
dramatically. He returned home to Decatur, Ga., and joined the "Jesus
people," a group of recovering addicts who studied and spread the word of
God.[6] He became so dedicated to religion that he constantly carried a Bible
with him, recorded his thoughts in a "Jesus notebook," and signed letters
with Biblical quotations.[7] Friends and family noticed the change immediately. "I was so relieved," Diane told *People*. "His behavior was so much
better. I mean, we could take him to see his grandparents again."

"It was a true personality split," said his childhood friend Miles Mc-
Manus. "He went into this Jesus Freak stage and his whole identity changed.
It was like he had to be the best Christian in the world."[8]

4   *People*, Feb. 23, 1987
5   Jones, p. 103
6   *People*, Feb. 23, 1987
7   New York, Dec. 20, 1980
8   Jones, p. 117

But there was fallout from his conversion. While he once had greatly enjoyed the music of John Lennon and the Beatles, his new philosophies and lifestyle placed him directly at odds with his idols—those who had claimed to be "more popular than Jesus." A friend told the Associated Press that Chapman had said, "Who the hell are they to be comparing themselves to Jesus?" Chapman now refused to play Beatles songs on his guitar, and it was John Lennon that became the focus of his anger. He told friends that John's new solo release "Imagine" was a "communist song," and that to "imagine there's no heaven" was blasphemy. Chapman, changing those lyrics, sang aloud, "imagine John Lennon is dead."[9]

Of course, that's not the type of behavior preached by Jesus in the Bible, which raises the question: Was Chapman's newfound religious conversion

The house where Mark David Chapman grew up in Decatur, Ga. In this house, at age 12, Chapman first told his mother of the kingdom of the Little People.

truly a gift from God? Or was it a tool to make him angry, given to him by the devil?

Also during this time, a friend introduced Chapman to the book *The Catcher in The Rye.* The novel tells the story of Holden Caulfield, a 16-year-old who is expelled from his preparatory school and then spends the next few days wandering the streets of New York City cynically pondering life. In the book's pivotal passage, Caulfield envisions himself at the edge of a cliff catching children who might otherwise fall off while playing. The falling children are symbolic of the transfer from adolescence to adulthood, a growth that is undesirable because, Caulfield says, adults are "phonies." Chapman became obsessed with the book and urged all his friends to read it.

9   Jones, p. 117

In the early 1970s, Chapman joined the South Dekalb County Young Men's Christian Association (YMCA) in Decatur. The kids were drawn to him and followed him wherever he went in camp. They nicknamed him "Nemo," after the mysterious captain in Jules Verne's *Twenty Thousand Leagues Under the Sea*. Once while receiving a "Counselor of the Year" award, all the kids in camp cheered "Nemo! Nemo! Nemo!"[10] (Chapman later told *Frontline* that he had liked having a nickname, until years later when he learned that "nemo," in Latin, means "nothing." He promptly stopped using the name.) Supervisors were so impressed that in 1975 they nominated Chapman for an assignment in Beirut, Lebanon, but the team was quickly evacuated when war broke out. Chapman was reassigned to work with the resettlement of Vietnamese refugees in Fort Chaffee, Ark. Moore, at the time a YMCA executive who was directing the resettlement, said, "He was one of the most compassionate staff members we had. He came to be a team coordinator, one of five in the entire camp. It was a pretty responsible job for a guy only 20 years old."[11]

Not everything was perfect with Chapman, though. The year was 1975, and there were still signs of inner turmoil. A YMCA colleague later told *People*: "One time in the music room a bunch of Laotians were playing our band instruments. Mark stood there with this funny expression on his face, and then finally went over and picked up a guitar and joined in. He played a really wild song—The Surfaris' tune 'Wipe Out'—and really got into it. When it was over he was really mad at himself. He told me, 'I don't ever want to do anything like that again. It takes me away from God.' He said he felt like the guitar had some kind of control over him."

Then in late summer, he lost his virginity to his female roommate, despite being engaged to Jessica Blankenship, a childhood friend from Georgia. Afterward his letters to Blankenship included statements such as "I'm so sinful and filthy," and "I'm constantly struggling with my identity," and "my ship is nearly sinking." Blankenship, a devout Christian, visited Fort Chaffee in October. "After that I think is when I first started noticing that

---

10   Jones, p. 124
11   *Chicago Sun-Times*, Dec. 10, 1980

he was just having a lot of struggles within himself," she told a friend. "It was like a big war was going on inside him."[12]

According to *Frontline*, "He was closer than ever to the children, still the Pied Piper, the cheerful organizer of camp games. But to his co-workers, he appeared tense, often moody, frequently depressed, a loner. To one friend, it seemed Mark had fallen out of grace with himself."

That friend was Cindy Newton, whom Chapman had embraced when she first came to camp as a scared nine-year-old. She loved Chapman for his kind and gentle nature. But later, that changed. She told *Frontline*, "He came to visit one time and he came into the kitchen and I started to run up to hug him, but his face looked different and his eyes were cold. And I backed off and Mom says, 'Aren't you going to go up and hug Mark?' And I kind of shook my head and said, 'He looks different.' And she says, 'It's the same old Mark.' But it wasn't the same old Mark. He had shark eyes and he had no feeling in his face. He looked very cold and very unhappy, and he scared me."

When Chapman left Fort Chaffee that fall, a friend from Atlanta, Dana Reeves, came to pick him up. A fellow worker remembered: "Dana had a long-barreled six-shooter. Mark was very excited showing it to us. He said it held really well in the hand." Another friend said: "Dana had a strange effect on Mark. He was older than Mark and rougher, and Mark seemed to be excited around him, but in a different way than I'd ever seen him."[13] Reeves would later become notably instrumental in furthering Chapman's fate.

After leaving the refugee camp, Chapman joined Blankenship at Covenant College in Tennessee, a Christ-centered institution committed to the Bible and the word of God. Together, they attended fundamentalist prayer groups that practiced charismatic Christianity, integrating mind, body and spirit into a full relationship with Jesus. Yet Chapman still grew darker. After one prayer session he told Jessica that he dreamed of making love to a prostitute in front of her, and that in class he daydreamed about life being all about dying and that history was all about war, destruction and death. Moreover, he'd thought about suicide.[14] "He just seemed lost," Blankenship

---

12   *People*, Feb. 23, 1987
13   *People*, June 22, 1981
14   *People*, Feb. 23, 1987

says in *Let Me Take You Down*, "like he didn't know what to do with himself." In 2005 she told *Dateline NBC* that she remembered Chapman would cry "quite a bit" over things she viewed as minor. "I mean, people cry every once in a while," she said. "But he seemed to be crying over things that to me didn't seem to be that big of a deal. ... He [had] sort of a dark side, I guess. And I just really didn't want to have anything to do with it. ... I was recognizing that he was emotionally unstable and I wanted to get out of the relationship, but I was afraid that he was going to kill himself." After just one semester, Chapman dropped out and moved back to Decatur.

At Reeves' suggestion, Chapman took a shooting-range test, scored 88 out of 100, and got a job as a security guard.[15] He armed his personal car with tear gas and a spotlight, and he carried his gun with him at all times. Blankenship had pictures of Chapman in his security uniform that she later destroyed. "He had this horrible expression on his face, like just a mean look," she told Jonathan Marks, Chapman's defense attorney in 1981.[16] Chapman didn't last long at the job, he and Blankenship broke up, and he decided to move to Hawaii and to kill himself. He even asked for help doing it; he later told Marks, "I began to pray to [Satan]."

On June 20, 1977, Chapman rented a car, purchased a vacuum cleaner hose and drove to a remote Honolulu beach. He fitted the hose to the exhaust pipe, ran it through the hatchback window and sealed the gap with old clothes. He climbed inside the car, closed the door, started the engine and sat back in his seat. He felt at peace, closed his eyes and waited to die. But 15 minutes later he awoke to a tapping on the window. Standing outside the car was a Japanese fisherman. The heat from the exhaust pipe had burnt a hole in the plastic hose leading inside the car. Chapman's suicide attempt had failed.[17]

Many Christians believe that even attempted suicide is a mortal sin, a most serious offense against God. Chapman was spared the finality of death, but in living, he still faced the dire consequence of having turned away from

---

15   *Newsweek*, Dec. 22, 1980
16   *People*, Feb. 23, 1987
17   *People*, Feb. 23, 1987

his maker. Through his own free will, he forfeited hope of redemption. Consequently, he was even more susceptible to the influence of evil.

In the case of Chapman, however, this sin was probably more effect than cause. According to Father Amorth, suicide is a severe symptom of possession. "This is the final goal of the evil enemy," he writes, "to bring us to despair and suicide." But the devil appeared to have different plans for Chapman. His suicide attempt did not free him from internal pain; it only compounded it. The destructiveness of his fear and anger just needed a target.

The day after his suicide attempt, Chapman sought help and checked into Castle Memorial Hospital in Kailua, Hawaii. His dark side was apparent to his caretakers. Jones writes: "When the psychiatrist asked him how he felt, Chapman answered with a dramatic metaphor of violence.

"'I think of myself as a boxer in the 27th round with my face all bloody, my teeth knocked out and my body all bruised,' he said.

"The doctor noted that the suicidal young man from Georgia 'actually looked tired as he expressed these feelings' but 'did not want to explore who or what he was fighting.'"

Though they didn't know it, Castle Memorial staff would be unable to help Chapman. Amorth makes clear that medical and psychiatric treatment are futile against demonic possession. But Chapman did have another turn of personality while admitted. In fact, he made what appeared to be a rapid and miraculous recovery, and hospital officials were so impressed with his progress that they offered him a full-time job at their facility. One of his supervisors, Leilani Siegfried, remembers how quickly Chapman made friends: "[Mark] would leave little notes with smile faces saying, 'Have a nice day' or 'Cheer up—life's not that bad,'" she told *People*. "All the patients, particularly the older ones that nobody else would talk to, just loved that boy, and I can't say enough good about him."

The good times continued, as Chapman fell in love with a Japanese-American girl named Gloria Abe. According to *People*, she was Buddhist, with an interest in the occult; she dappled in astrology, graphology and tarot-card reading. In January of 1979, Chapman proposed marriage, and on June 2 they were wed. But before long, Abe, too, began noticing oddities in Chapman's behavior. He began drinking regularly and stopped going to church. He purged their life of what he decided were needless material possessions—books, kitchen utensils, records, Abe's jewelry and guitar, their car—just to replace some shortly afterward. He spoke of disappearing from society, and he would stay awake into the early hours of morning. Laying in bed, she would hear him in the next room making anonymous threatening phone calls to his former landlord, to a TV repairman, to a doctor at Castle Hospital.[18] He also acted out toward Abe. Jones explains how Chapman would throw away her possessions, or break them, or push her against a wall, or spit on her, or hit her—for an offense as minor as mildly criticizing him. There was also behavior Abe didn't see. Chapman made upward of 40 calls a day to a local church and whispered, "Bang, bang, you're dead."[19] He phoned the Ili Kai Hotel with a bomb threat and watched the evacuation from across the street. He memorized the number of the pay phone opposite their apartment window, and he would call passersby and say he was stalking them and would kill them.[20]

He became interested in lithography and frequented numerous art galleries. This, too, quickly became an obsession. He began buying pieces of artwork—a serigraph by Hero Yamagata, a $5,000 gold wall plaque of Salvador Dali's "Lincoln in Dalivision," a $7,500 lithograph of Norman Rockwell's "Triple Self-Portrait"—and had them expensively framed.[21] "I'm sure it occupied almost all his time," Pat Carlson, a saleswoman at one of the galleries Chapman patronized, told UPI. "[He] spent a fortune on telephone calls to the mainland, checking things, researching things. ... I always felt sorry for his wife because I thought, My God, this guy is spending his life in galleries."

His art fixation drew him into painting his own pictures, which further revealed the darkness inside him. Jones writes that Abe marveled at Chap-

---

18   *People*, March 2, 1987
19   *Newsweek*, Dec. 22, 1980
20   Jones, p. 206-7
21   *People*, March 2

man's talent, believing he had a gift for painting exquisite scenes. "But it seemed he could never leave them alone," she said. "He just kept going back and going back over and over them until these beautiful watercolors became a mass of blackness. It was like nothing he did was ever good enough until he destroyed it."

In late winter of 1980, Chapman suddenly lost interest in art and switched his obsession to eliminating financial liabilities. He dubbed his new plan "Operation Freedom from Debt." Abe remembered him sitting quietly alone, hour after hour, day after day, working morning, afternoon or evening with pencil and calculator, as if he needed to settle his finances in time for an important imminent event. According to *People*, "his calendar for the period is a barely legible grid of crossings-out, the written record of his immersion in a wallow of details. … Plainly, to him, more than money was at stake."

Fortunately for Chapman, he did receive help on his new quest: The Little People returned. In his decade of absence, they had shed the shackles of monarchy and become more organized, creating a democracy rife with committees charged with reorganizing the life of their president, Mark David Chapman. "Before making any decisions," Jones writes, "especially regarding finances, [Chapman] subjected his proposals to the review of cabinet officers, various committees, and then to a congressional body for approval, rejections, or further deliberation."

Chapman's obsessions continued to oscillate. According to *People*, his interests in 1980 changed direction as follows:

> **March 13:** Operation Freedom from Debt commences, and, having declared sugar evil, Chapman enjoys a diet free of the sweetener.

> **April 7:** He decides to make a hobby of filming home movies, using Abe's 8mm camera.

> **April 15:** He gives up drinking hard liquor.

April 23: He abandons his diet and starts another, quits film-making and later sells Abe's camera.

May 11: He modifies his hard-liquor rule to allow for drinking away from home, and again abandons his diet for new eating regulations.

June: He scours music stores to replace his collection of Todd Rundgren albums that he had previously purged.

July: He sells the Rundgren collection because, Abe says, "it depressed him to hear music that good."

August: Finally free of debt, he purchases a Sony Walkman. The next day he returns it and buys speakers for his record player. Two days later he smashes his turntable with a hammer, then throws away his television set so he will no longer be "manipulated by it."

Chapman continued to grow to hate the world around him. In September, he took his mother to visit the Pearl Harbor memorial. As the tour boat passed the sunken ship *Arizona*, people began throwing flowers into the water; but Chapman, instead of feeling melancholy or reverent, began to laugh. "My mother looked at me and was shocked," he says in *Let Me Take You Down*. "I couldn't explain why I laughed. I didn't think it was funny or anything. It's just that I was unable to feel sympathy or grief, the human emotion that I was supposed to feel."

By October of 1980, Chapman was experiencing insomnia, migraine headaches and night sweats. He was paranoid and angry. He told his wife, "Sometimes I get so frustrated and bottled up I just want to blow somebody's head off."[22]

And then he felt the presence of demons.

---

22   *People*, March 2

"Have you ever woken up from a deep sleep with the sensation that some-thing evil is in the room?" Chapman asked later. "You're not really awake, but you're not really dreaming, either. Your eyes won't open more than about halfway. You just feel paralyzed with a fear that's so powerful you don't know who you are. You're so frightened you've virtually lost your identity. ... You try to scream but nothing comes out, just all this fear holding you down in your bed so you can't move. You can't even scream. My whole life was like that at that time, a half-waking nightmare."[23]

Chapman said the only place he was able to find peace was in the Hono-lulu Public Library.[24] Perhaps he felt tranquil there because that's where his demons wanted him to be. It was amongst those shelves that he thought again of his old favorite book, *The Catcher in the Rye*. "It just came to my mind to see if it was there," he said. He discovered it was checked out and overdue, and after re-checking week after week, he finally bought a new copy from a bookstore and read it twice again. He once again became angry at the pho-niness of humanity, and lashed out in his imagination, and began to think about someone to kill.

"My mind is disheveled. It's ripped and torn," he said later, reflecting on his feelings in the fall of 1980. "There is a tornado in my mind, circling around my brain, bits and pieces crashing into the walls. A debris. Broken things. Cloudy things. Things I can't see, bits and pieces of memories like pieces of torn photographs just blowing across my mind. But at all times, at the forefront, the big, black cloud of the tornado. The hurt—the hurt, the frustration, the lack of esteem. And always, constantly, a loud, spiritual noise, echoing through my being, just ripping apart anything that I would try to build to get myself out of the maelstrom."[25]

His fate, though, was that only murder would get him out. He later told a psychologist and his legal counsel that he had considered targeting the gov-ernor of Hawaii, or Johnny Carson, or Jackie Onassis, or Paul McCartney, or Elizabeth Taylor, or George C. Scott, or Ronald Reagan. The library held the answer to his dilemma. One day while perusing the biography section, "not

23   Jones, p. 169
24   Jones, p. 167
25   Jones, p. 174-5

After Mark David Chapman saw John Lennon's biography *One Day at a Time*, he believed that Lennon was a phony.

looking for any book in particular," he said, Chapman came across *John Lennon, One Day at a Time* by Anthony Fawcett. On the cover was a picture of John in New York City, standing at the base of the Statue of Liberty, wearing his dark sunglasses with a cap and a scarf around his neck. Chapman read that John was living a comfortable life in an expensive co-op apartment in Manhattan's desirable Upper West Side, and that he was a stay-at-home dad who dotingly cared for his nearly 5-year-old son. Paging through the book, Chapman came across pictures of John standing on the roof of the Dakota dressed in a black outfit and wearing a sign on his lapel that read "Elvis." While looking at those pictures, Chapman's mind became filled with anger. What a big phony, he thought. Here stood the man who preached to the world about love, peace, giving and helping, and now he's living a luxurious life in one of the most extravagant buildings in New York City. "Just as Holden Caulfield had bled through the ink of *Catcher* and entered my mind, John Lennon entered my mind through that book," Chapman said. "That was when the winds that were swirling across my mind reached a fever pitch and swallowed up the few remaining fragments of decency and free will I had left. That was when I turned so vile that my own mind vomited me into the pits of hell."[26]

---

26   Jones, p. 177

When Mark David Chapman saw this photo from the inside of *Sgt. Pepper,* he decided to kill John Lennon.

Chapman did nothing to avert his evil thoughts; through his actions he nurtured them, even welcomed them in. He spent his nights reading *Catcher,* looking at pictures of John Lennon, listening to Beatles albums. In Jones' book, Gloria remembers trying to sleep in the next room, but Chapman keeping her awake the whole night. She would hear him calling out John's name, talking in voices she had never heard before, saying, "the phony bastard must die" and "the catcher in the rye is coming for you" and "imagine John Lennon is dead, oh yeah, yeah, yeah." She was struck motionless, frightened to leave the room for fear of who or what she might see.

Then, finally, the decisive moment came. "I remember opening up the *Sgt. Pepper* album and seeing that bright yellow photograph of all four Beatles in their fluorescent DayGlo army uniforms," Chapman said. "There's Lennon with his glasses and his little moustache. As soon as I saw his picture on that album, I remember thinking—I thought ... I knew—that I was going to kill him."[27]

Chapman intently listened to his inner demon; the sounds of "Lucy in the Sky with Diamonds" reverberated through his headphones, and he prayed to the devil. "Slowly, ritualistically, he began removing his clothes," Jones writes.

---

27   Jones, p. 179

"At last he sat before the record player, naked except for a pair of headphones clamped across his skull.

"'Hear me, Satan,' he prayed softly, bowing his head. 'Accept these pearls of my evil and my rage. Accept these things from deep within me. In return, I ask only that you ...'

"He paused, lifting the headphones momentarily from his head to assure himself that his wife was still asleep behind the closed door in the next room. A chill passed through his body.

"'I ask only that you give me the power,' he continued, rocking gently in time to the Lennon song, ... 'the power to kill John Lennon. Give me the power of darkness. Give me the power of death. Let me be somebody for once in my life. Give me the life of John Lennon.'"

On October 23, 1980, John ended a five-year retreat from public life and released the solo single "Just Like Starting Over." On the same day, Chapman quit his job, signed the security ledger "John Lennon," and then crossed out the signature.

Four days later, Chapman visited a Honolulu gun shop and purchased a Charter Arms .38 snubnosed revolver with a five-bullet cylinder. On October 29, he boarded a plane for New York. He checked into the exclusive Waldorf-Astoria on Park Avenue and started a high-priced tour of the city: He embarked on a boat trip around Manhattan, and a helicopter ride over it; he attended theater presentations and ate in expensive restaurants. After a couple of days at the Waldorf, he moved to the Olcott Hotel on 72nd Street, just a few doors from John's Dakota apartment building. Then he began his stakeout. For hours he waited in front of the Dakota, but the Beatle never appeared.

John's absence was irrelevant anyway; Chapman had no bullets. He had tried to buy some in Manhattan but was turned away due to strict ammunition laws in New York state. Undeterred, he flew to Atlanta to visit Reeves, who was working as a sheriff's deputy. Chapman explained that he was visiting New York and needed a few rounds for self-protection; Reeves gave him five hollow-point bullets, which are more accurate than standard bullets and explode inside a body after impact. The pair went target shooting in the woods, then Chapman left for Manhattan on November 9.

Then fate—or a more calculated, sinister force—influenced Chapman even further. On the plane back to New York, he noticed the most recent issue of *Esquire* in a magazine rack.[28] The cover photo was of John Lennon. The publication and content of the article could not have been more timely. The writer, Laurence Shames, recorded his search for the old Lennon of the 1960s and the peace-pushing Lennon of the 70s, the man "who had always taken chances" musically and politically, the man who "by his unflinching slit-eyed stare, by his appalling honesty, had shamed the world into examining itself." Instead he found "false leads, dead ends, witnesses about as credible as hair-restore ads"—and no John Lennon. After untold hours of research, though, Shames laments he is glad the search failed: "The Lennon I would have found is a 40-year-old businessman who watches a lot of television, who's got $150 million, a son whom he dotes on, and a wife who intercepts his phone calls. He's got good lawyers to squeeze him through tax loopholes, and he's learned the political advantages of silence." What Shames did find were John's four mansions, his 16,000 acres of land in New York's Catskill Mountains, his yacht and some of his 250 Holstein cows (minus the one that had recently sold for $265,000). The story was a harsh judgment of a man who heartily joined the establishment and was living a comfortable life in the 28 rooms he owned in the exclusive Dakota apartments. Chapman's feelings were affirmed.

But once back in New York, he again saw no signs of John, and he began to doubt his plan. He called his wife and confessed the intentions of his trip. "I was as gentle as I could be to him," she told *People*. "I did not want to say something that would change his mind [again]. I said … it was over now and he should just come home."

Chapman did return to Hawaii, but not for long. Over the next few weeks he couldn't get John Lennon off his mind. Finally, he told his wife he was leav-

---

28   Jones, p. 199

ing to look for a new career, and on Saturday, December 6, 1980, he arrived back in Manhattan to carry out his original plan. He checked into the YMCA on 63rd Street, near Central Park West, nine blocks from the Dakota. He renewed his stakeout that day; for hours he waited, but John never appeared. Eventually Chapman gave up and left for dinner and a movie. The following day he checked into the Sheraton Center, room 2730. He unpacked his bags and set out on the dresser the few possessions that he had brought with him.

He later told a psychiatrist that on the evening of December 7, alone in his hotel room, he "summoned devils from high places."[29] Mark David Chapman, or the force dwelling inside him, was ready to kill John Lennon.

---

29   United Press International, Aug. 24, 1981

It Was 20 Years Ago Today

For everything there is a season,
And a time for every matter under heaven.
A time to be born and a time to die.
A time to plant and a time to pluck up what is planted.
A time to kill and a time to heal.
— Ecclesiastes 3

John Lennon knew what was coming. In the final year and months before his death, he became a man acutely aware of his own fate, a man filled with fear, frightened of his own future.

In his book *The Last Days of John Lennon*, Frederic Seaman discusses the Beatle's fascination with mysticism, magic and his earthly demise. "He talked about his death early on from the context of books he'd been reading," Seaman writes. "He was always reading about the occult and about death. All this stuff was totally foreign to me. So I tried to just space out when he was talking about it because I didn't want to deal with it. It wasn't until later, after months and months of this, that I realized this was a big deal in his life and he really spent a lot of energy obsessing about this."

Seaman's uncle, Norman, had been shot in New York City in 1978, and survived. "The bullet just sort of went in and out. It wasn't a big deal," Seaman says in Jack Jones' book *Let Me Take You Down*. "But every time my uncle Norman and John would get together, John would always ask him about getting shot. 'What was it like? What went through your mind? What went through your head? What did it feel like? Did you see the bullet?'

"And my uncle would say, 'Well, it felt like an ice pick going into your flesh.' And John would sit there wide-eyed. He just, like, hung on every word."

In the last months of his life, John passed several weeks with Seaman on vacation in Bermuda. They'd spend evenings sitting on the terrace of a rented shorefront house, looking over the water, smoking marijuana and listening to reggae music. It was on these evenings that John would ruminate on his grim obsession. "There were many conversations," Seaman writes. "Particularly when he was stoned; that's where his mind would gravitate toward, which was always very disturbing to me because that's the last thing I wanted to talk about. I just wanted to listen to the Bob Marley that John was always playing then. I didn't want to hear John talk about death. It always freaked me out. ... I find it interesting with retrospect that he became more and more obsessed. He talked about it more and more as his approach to New York neared. ... He talked as if he had some kind of rendezvous with something, you know?"

One specific night stands prominent in Seaman's memory. The sun had set as he and John were sitting and looking out over the ocean. Seaman writes: "[John] loaded Marley's latest release, *Uprising*, into the tape player. We sat in silence for a long time, taking in Marley's hypnotic music. The last piece on the tape, titled 'Redemption Song,' was an acoustic ballad eerily reminiscent of some of John's demos. As the song ended, John got up and stood at the edge of the terrace. I stole a sideways glance at his face, which was illuminated faintly by the moon, giving it a ghostly pallor. John motioned me to stand next to him.

"'Well, Fred,' he said, placing his arm around my shoulder, "I guess it's time to say good-bye to paradise.' I was surprised by his intimate gesture. Standing silently in the moonlight, listening to the waves lapping at the foot of the terrace, I felt close to John. I sensed that his heart was heavy and I wished there were a way to ease his pain.

"He took one last fierce drag on his Gitane and then tossed the cigarette butt into the dark waters. John abruptly walked back to the house, leaving me to ponder his strange behavior as I stood frozen at the edge of the terrace. Although I had grown accustomed to his morbid talk, there was something profoundly disturbing in John's solemn demeanor that night."

What, specifically, had caused John's heart to become heavy that evening? It might have been the messages in Marley's lyrics, which John may have interpreted to be speaking directly to him. Aside from "Redemption Song," a previous track on the album, "Zion Train," carried an even stronger message. It calls for people to "get on board, ... the soul train is coming our way." The lyrics are clear in regard to John's life:

> *Which man can save his brother's soul?*
> *Oh man, it's just self control.*
> *Don't gain the world and lose your soul.*
> *Wisdom is better than silver and gold.*

In John's final days in the recording studio in 1980, he once again talked of his own death, confiding in Jack Douglas, the producer of the album *Double Fantasy*. Albert Goldman writes of one noteworthy conversation: "Before the session ended, during a period when Yoko was out of the studio, John leaned back against the tape machine, where he had delivered so many monologues during the past four months, and said to Jack: 'Don't repeat to Yoko what I'm going to tell you.' Then he went into the same rap that he had laid on Fred. ... John said that his days were numbered and that he was living on borrowed time. He didn't allude to assassination, but he appeared completely resigned to dying. He even discussed what would happen to his legend after his death, boasting that he would become much more famous than Elvis. Jack had heard Lennon speak of death before—but never with the sense of its imminence that he conveyed that night."

In one of John's last compositions, he begins to show remorse for what he had done and anxiety about what lay in his future. The song, titled "Help Me to Help Myself," was released almost 20 years after his death, on October 9, 2000. The song is a haunting, moving prayer to God:

> *Well, I tried so hard to stay alive,*
> *But the angel of destruction keeps on hounding me all around.*
> *But I know in my heart that we never really parted, oh no.*
>
> *They say the Lord helps those who help themselves.*
> *So I'm asking this question in the hope that you'll be kind.*
> *'Cause I know deep inside I was never satisfied, oh no.*
>
> *Lord, help me. Lord, help me now. Please help me, Lord.*
> *Help me to help myself.*
> *Help me to help myself.*

In the final moments of the song, John can be heard talking in a faint voice, saying, "I see, I see. That's how you're going to do it. Huh, O.K."

Even Yoko, at least in retrospect, sensed something foreboding in the lyrics. Of the song, she told London's *The Independent*: "They say that people start to think of God near death. It's possible that was the case here."

By Monday, December 8, 1980, the evil that had subtly infiltrated Mark David Chapman's life had fully engulfed him, and he had grown to recognize and reconcile with his indwelling spirit. Unlike other times, on this day he felt comforted. The uncertainty as to what his next step should be was gone. The multitude of conflicting emotions had ceased and he was now the obedient executioner. The spiritual battle between good and evil that had raged within him his whole life reached its day of decision. He would soon commit an act of murder, perhaps for the spiritual claiming of a soul. God may have called out to Chapman to relent, but in Chapman's dreadful ignorance, he would have scarcely heard through the tumult in his mind. And for John, if 20 years earlier he had indeed sold his soul, then he had greatly betrayed God, and in this matter, God would not show him mercy. From this impending hell upon earth there was no escape; each man was likely held captive by forces of evil—Chapman by coercion, Lennon by choice.

In his room at the Sheraton Center that Monday morning, Chapman was nearly clairvoyant, sensing that would be the day he would become an assassin. "I woke up knowing, somehow, that when I left that room, that was the last time I would see that room again," he says in *Let Me Take You Down.* "I truly felt in my bones. I don't know how. I had never seen John Lennon up to that point … but I somehow knew that this was it, this was the day."

Chapman realized that sleuths would later visit the hotel, looking for clues about his past. So he created a display on the dresser, carefully arranging certain articles of interest. Of particular significance, he laid open a Bible to reveal the Gospel of St. John, the title of which he changed to "… John Lennon." He also left behind his passport; an 8-track tape containing his favorite music by Todd Rundgren; a picture from his favorite movie, *The Wizard of Oz,* showing Dorothy wiping a tear from the cowardly lion's face; photographs of himself with Vietnamese children; and a letter from his YMCA supervisor commending him on his outstanding work with refugees. He hoped the items would help define his life to the world, that they would be an answer to those he knew would race to judge him, that they would portray a picture of better days when he felt fulfilled. He wanted to explain that he was not totally to blame for his deed. His violent act was not one man pronouncing judgment on another.

He stood alone in the quiet of his room, amid the noise in his mind. He withdrew five hollow-point bullets from his pocket. He knew they would increase their destructive power when they struck soft tissue—they would damage his victim's body more than other revolver ammunition would. He inserted the bullets into the cylinder of the gun he had purchased specifically to kill John Lennon, and proclaimed, "The catcher in the rye of my generation, Chapter 27."[1] And the heavy-set, confused man from Georgia hobbled onto the busy sidewalks of New York City.

First Chapman visited a store to purchase a new copy of *The Catcher in the Rye*, the book he'd been basing his philosophy on, the book he'd been living within, the book that could well have been a guide from the devil on how to carry out his plan. "The pages and sentences of that book were flowing through my brain and entering my blood, influencing my thoughts and actions," he tells Jones. "My very soul was breathing between the pages of *The Catcher in the Rye*." For a time, Chapman actually believed he had become Holden Caulfield.

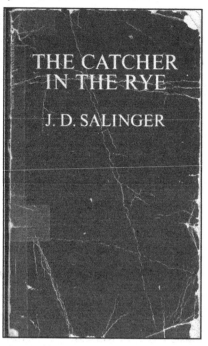

The Catcher in the Rye was a guide for Mark David Chapman.

Indeed, Chapman's story during his last few days in society closely mirrors Caulfield's. Both take place in Manhattan over a three-day weekend, beginning on Saturday and ending on Monday, during the month of December, approximately two weeks before Christmas. Chapman later told Jones that he re-read the novel in prison and that even he was startled at the number of similarities:

> Caulfield fails out of Pencey Prep School. He feels alienated from society and is unable to face his family with his failure. He wanders the streets of New York City on the verge of nervous collapse. After high school, Chapman enrolls in South DeKalb Community College but quickly drops out. In 1976, he at-

---

1   Jones, p. 21

tends Covenant College in Tennessee, where he quickly loses his identity and feels embarrassed that he can't keep pace with the younger students in his classes;[2] he leaves after one semester.

Caulfield wears a red hunting hat that he says makes him look corny, "like a screwball or something." Chapman wears "a Russian-style brimless hat with synthetic fur."[3]

Caulfield asks a taxi driver about the ducks in the lagoon near Central Park South: "By any chance, do you happen to know where they go, the ducks, when it gets all frozen over?" Chapman asks a police officer near Central Park, "Do you know where the ducks go in the winter?" The police officer just turns and walks away.[4]

Caulfield checks into the Edmont Hotel, a cheap place with a "crumby room" where he can't see anything out his window "except the other side of the hotel." Chapman checks into what he calls a "dingy room" at the YMCA. The mattress is thin, lumpy, and squeaky; he turns on the TV set and gets nothing but static. He feels depressed.[5]

Caulfield hires a prostitute to come to his hotel room. She wears a green dress. He notices that she's "very nervous, for a prostitute," and he does not have sex with her. Chapman has a prostitute come to his room at the Sheraton the evening before killing John; she wears a green dress, and is nervous, paranoid that she was followed. He does not have sex with her.[6]

Caulfield gets into an argument over money with the bellboy, Maurice, who had arranged for the prostitute. Holden envisions

---

2   Jones, p. 179
3   Jones, p. 8
4   Jones, p. 194
5   Jones, p. 11
6   Jones, p. 16

himself walking down the steps into the lobby carrying a gun and aiming it at Maurice, who pleads for mercy. "But I'd plug him anyway. Six shots right through his fat hairy belly." Chapman awakes during the night because he hears voices in the next room. He's furious when he realizes that they're men talking about having sex with other men. He imagines barging in to "shoot them all."[7]

Sitting in his hotel room, Caulfield thinks about committing suicide. "I felt like jumping out the window," he says. Then he mentions that he doesn't want "a bunch of stupid rednecks looking at me when I was all gory." Chapman thinks about suicide, perhaps by jumping off the top of the Statue of Liberty because nobody had ever done it that way before. He envisions his body lying at the bottom, covered with blood. "I imagined my brains hanging out and me still being alive," he says later.[8]

Caulfield sees a Broadway play and then a movie at Radio City Music Hall. Chapman does the same.

Visiting his old teacher, Mr. Antolini, Caulfield has a bad experience. Chapman visits an old high-school chorus teacher, Madison Short. He is happy to see her, but is upset when she is not friendly to him.[9]

Mr. Antolini tells Caulfield, "This fall I think you're riding for— it's a special kind of fall, a horrible kind. The man falling isn't permitted to feel or hear himself hit bottom. He just keeps falling and falling. The whole arrangement's designed for men who, at some time or other in their lives, were looking for something their own environment couldn't supply them with. So they gave

7   NBC Dateline, Nov. 18, 2005
8   Jones, p. 77
9   Jones, p. 197

up looking. They gave it up before they ever really even got start-ed." After Chapman buys the copy of *Catcher* on the morning of December 8, he randomly opens the book to that very passage. He notes the "synchronicity."[10]

Caulfield feels sickened by phony people. "I'd have this rule that nobody could do anything phony when they visited me," he says. "If anybody tried to do anything phony, they couldn't stay." At 25, Chapman begins to view himself as an another adult phony, and he views John as the biggest phony of them all. "The phony must die, says the catcher in the rye," he says. "Don't believe in John Lennon. The fool. The goddamn phony fool. He doesn't even realize that soon he's going to be dead."[11]

Caulfield gets upset with himself thinking about inappropriate responses he has toward people and personal events. Chapman reads the front page of a New York newspaper that mentions Pearl Harbor, and he thinks about his response from when he visited the memorial, having laughed while seeing and hearing about the destruction. He admits it was an inappropriate reac-tion, feels embarrassed and thinks, What's wrong with me?[12]

On his last day in New York City, Caulfield wakes up early and feels very depressed. He says, "It was Monday and all, and pretty near Christmas." When Chapman reads the book on the morn-ing of Monday, December 8, he randomly opens to the page containing that passage. He reads the words and notices that they describe his exact scenario. It sends a chill through his body.[13]

The novel ends with Caulfield at the carrousel in Central Park with his sister Phoebe. Chapman visits the same carrousel. Later

---

10   Jones, p. 22
11   Jones, p. 189
12   Jones, p. 13
13   Jones, p. 22

he admits to thinking of John Lennon's song "Watching the Wheels" from *Double Fantasy*, in which John sings that he's "no longer riding on the merry-go-round."[14]

Caulfield talks to Phoebe about the Robert Burns poem "Coming Through the Rye," which was the inspiration for Salinger's title for the novel. "I keep picturing all these little kids playing some game in this big field of rye and all," Holden says. "Thousands of little kids, and nobody's around—nobody big, I mean—except me. And I'm standing on the edge of some crazy cliff. What I have to do, I have to catch everybody if they start to go over the cliff—I mean if they're running and they don't look where they're going I have to come out from somewhere and catch them. That's all I'd do all day. I'd just be the catcher in the rye and all." As a dedicated social worker at the YMCA, Chapman begins to view himself as the catcher in the rye. The love and pain he feels for the children at the Vietnamese resettlement camp overwhelms him. At his sentencing for the murder of John Lennon, Chapman reads that same passage to the judge and court.

In killing John, Chapman believed he was taking the story of the 26-chapter novel to its conclusion; as mentioned earlier, he referred to his actions as "Chapter 27." Even in the weeks after the murder, he would use his trial as a vehicle to promote the book. He would carry copies with him constantly, and would sign and give them to prison guards and fellow inmates, to his lawyers and psychiatrists. He would tell everyone that if they read *The Catcher in the Rye* they would come to understand why he shot John Lennon.

Chapman left the store with his new copy of the novel and paused at the sidewalk to inscribe the opening page. "*This* is my statement," he wrote, and he signed it, "Holden Caulfield, the catcher in the rye."[15]

---

14   Frontline, Nov. 28, 1995
15   Jones, p. 22

He walked toward the Dakota, carrying a copy of *Double Fantasy* so that he would appear to be just another anxious fan in search of an autograph. Sitting across 72nd Street from the building, he became overwhelmed with visions of John standing on the roof taunting him. The pain that he felt wasn't going away. Chapman interpreted John's life as one of an evil man who neglected to live by his own words, a man who stubbornly followed his own will and who had fallen to every ill that he had so passionately preached to the rest of his generation to avoid. This, Chapman thought, was going to be his day to strike down John's phoniness. He would spoil and seize every one of John's earthly pleasures by taking his life. John Lennon was a big phony, and as an incarnation of Holden Caulfield, Chapman couldn't turn away from his duty. When second thoughts entered his mind, he prayed to his inner demons. "Please give me the strength," he pleaded. "The phonies have to know. It's pure, it's holy, it's real, and I can no longer stand this pain."[16]

He crossed the street and waited.

Lingering in the stone archway of the Dakota, Chapman was barraged with symbolism that supported his cause. He was struck by the grandeur of the structure, built in 1881 in a Gothic architectural style. Time had blackened its appearance, making it appear ominous.

And surrounding the building at street level were gargoyles—which are, writes author Bill Yenne in *Gothic Gargoyles*, "fallen rebel angels, demons forever condemned to the outside of buildings, never allowed to enter the interior." Gargoyles are thought to represent the struggle between Christian and pagan ideals, or between good and evil, vice and virtue; they symbolize Christianity standing against the occultists and the pagan gods and witches. Gargoyles were also thought to act as "spiritual scarecrows," Yenne writes, "intended to scare away the devil with a taste of his own gruesomeness." John may have hoped that one day they would offer him protection from the forces that he knew would come calling.

According to Jones, Chapman also knew the Dakota was used as the backdrop for Roman Polanski's film version of Ira Levin's novel *Rosemary's Baby*,

---

16   Jones, p. 27

The seventh floor of the Dakota on the west side of New York City was not only the home of John Lennon and Yoko Ono, but the was also the exact building and floor as the home of Guy and Rosemary Woodhouse in the film *Rosemary's Baby*, which incidentally depicted a deal with the devil.

a tale of a young woman who gives birth to the son of Satan. Not only was the film location uncanny, but the plot itself was somewhat prophetic. A young, newly married couple, Guy and Rosemary Woodhouse, relocate to an apartment in New York City. The couple is warned before moving in that the building has a notorious, sordid and unsavory reputation as a stage for witchcraft. Then Guy, an unemployed actor, makes a deal with the devil: For advancing his acting career, Guy allows Satan to secretly impregnate his wife. In the film, the Woodhouses live on the seventh floor—the same as John and Yoko. In another irony Chapman was aware of, Polanski had been a character in his own real-life occult story within a year of directing the film. His pregnant wife, actress Sharon Tate, was terrorized and stabbed to death by followers of Charles Manson (whom they sometimes referred to as "Satan") obeying what they believed was a secret message received through a Beatles song.[17]

Chapman thought the confluence of these symbols was too impeccable to be coincidence. Then, at the moment he was thinking all this, he noticed a woman walk past him, cross the street and disappear into Central Park; it was Mia Farrow, who had portrayed Rosemary in Polanski's film. Chapman needed no further confirmation. "It has to be right," he said to himself. "This has to be the day."[18]

Unforeseen powers were almost surely in action, and the Dakota and its players stood small and vulnerable to the assaults of the supernatural. So

---

17   Bugliosi, p. 414
18   Jones, p. 28

Chapman stood his guard outside the building. He began reading *Catcher* again. Then a taxi pulled to the curb, the door opened, and John Lennon stepped out. He shut the door behind him and walked inside the building. Chapman, deeply caught within the pages of his favorite novel, never even saw him. He was only aware once the doorman asked if he'd noticed.

Chapman felt disappointed, but sensed that he would get another opportunity. "This wasn't the right time anyway," he said to himself. "When the time is right it will happen. He'll be back. It won't be long now. I got a feeling."[19]

As the day progressed, other Beatles fans arrived. One was a woman named Jude, whom Chapman had befriended the previous day; another was a freelance photographer named Paul Goresh. Later, as they stood in front of the Dakota, a young child holding the hand of an elderly woman came from within the archway; it was Sean Lennon, John and Yoko's son, accompanied by his nanny. Chapman walked over to see the boy, and Jude, who knew the nanny, introduced them. Chapman knelt before Sean, released his grip on the revolver in his pocket, and reached out to shake the boy's hand. "I came all the way across the ocean from Hawaii," Chapman said, "and I'm honored to meet you."[20] They all stood watching as the pair climbed into an awaiting car and rode away. John was inside talking with RKO radio, giving his last interview.

Jude decided to depart, leaving only Goresh and Chapman. In midafternoon, a small group exited the building, none of them appearing to be important to Chapman's cause. Then suddenly, behind them, appeared John and Yoko. Chapman stood frozen as John and his entourage waited for a cab. His idol—his target—stood right before him in the wavering light of a winter afternoon. Chapman did nothing.

He just stood, a man with a mission and a revolver, motionless and thoughtless at the edge of his destiny. Perhaps time was slowing a bit. Perhaps God was laying His own hand on the scene, offering Chapman a reprieve from the chatter of his demons. Either way, the mood of the moment suddenly changed.

---

19   Jones, p. 29
20   Jones, p. 31

Goresh nudged him. "Paul started pushing me," Chapman later told *People* magazine. "He says, 'Go. There he is.' And Paul started taking his pictures. And I went up to him and I said, 'John, would you sign my album please?' He said, 'Sure,' and he signed it and he looked at me very earnestly and very sincerely in my eyes."

Meekly, Chapman held the album in his outstretched hand. John squinted and smiled, took the album, and gestured for Chapman's pen. As Chapman watched, spellbound, the rock 'n' roll icon scribbled to get the ink flowing, chuckled, and then signed "John Lennon, 1980." Chapman's hands hung limp as John smiled again and gave him back the autographed album.

Chapman just stared.

"Is ..." John hesitated mid-thought, looking back at Chapman, perhaps sensing something amiss, something sinister, something ominous. Then he finished his question: "Is that all you want?"

Slowly Chapman took the album and pen from John's hands. "Thanks," he said. "Thanks, John." And for a moment in his former hero's presence, Chapman's anger left him. He stood mystified, with no hostility.[21]

But the peace didn't last. The demons within would not allow Chapman to turn back for good. Jones reports that Chapman began hearing contradicting voices in his head, one of a child telling him, "You can have him now," and one of an adult screaming "No!"—and the child continuing, "Put your hand in your pocket. He's yours. He's mine. You promised! You bastard! Phony bastard! You promised!" The voices reverberated in Chapman's consciousness as John disappeared into a limousine and was whisked away.

Chapman noted that stars don't usually date their signatures. And suddenly he started having thoughts of dismissing the idea of murdering John, going back to his hotel, checking out, taking a cab to the airport and flying home.[22]

But abandonment of the plan was not meant to be. The arms of evil would not allow him to turn away. A pawn was in place, ready to strike, and it would not be forfeited.

Chapman continued to wait outside the Dakota.

---

21   Jones, p. 36
22   Jones, p. 37

At 8 p.m., Goresh decided to leave for his home in New Jersey, and Chapman begged him to stay. "You really ought to wait a while longer," he said. "Suppose you don't see him again. ... Suppose something happens to him."[23] But Goresh did depart and Chapman was left with only the night doorman, José Perdomo. Chapman sensed what was happening, but he stood helpless to stop it. He told *People*, "It's like ... the actors were there—me, José, the girl and Paul—and one by one it was their turn to exit, although I wanted them to stay. And then it started getting darker and the wind was whipping up that street. It was very eerie. I knew it was going to happen."

Chapman lay in wait with a dire feeling, knowing that in a few hours his identity would be altered forever; whenever John Lennon was thought of, Chapman would be, too. As the day declined and the shadows of the evening deepened, the thoughts of murder seized Chapman's mind that much stronger. Whatever was happening to him was now beyond his control. He prayed, but his prayer was divided: half to God, half to Satan—half to leave, half to slay.[24]

Chapman was very aware of the spiritual conflict within and around him. He tells Jones about his bisected feelings in those last hours, about his struggle between good and evil, characterized by an inner adult and an inner child: "The spiritual dichotomy: devil-God. And the inner dichotomy: the child-the man. They're out there in front of the Dakota late at night, long after everybody else but the doorman has gone away. They're cold, and the adult wants to go home. Even this phony, disheveled, shaking, trembling-inside adult wants to go home—just go home and show the autograph, John Lennon's autograph, to his wife.

"'Get the first cab out of here. Ask that doorman to get you a cab,' [the adult says].

"Then the child screams: 'No! No! No! ... I want to kill him. I want to kill him. He's mine! I want him.

"Then the adult: 'God help me! Save me, God, from this. Help me. Get me out of here.'

---

23   Jones, p. 41
24   *People*, March 2, 1987

"'No, no, no. Devil! Help me, devil! Give me the power and the strength to do this. … Please. I want this I want this so bad. I want this so bad.'"

Plenty of help was there. In the street and buildings surrounding the darkened archway on 72nd Street, one can imagine the demons gathered in great numbers, a gallery of spectators to behold the victory, to observe the last remaining moments of a man whose soul was owed to Satan.

Shortly before 11 o'clock, a white limousine appeared in the distance, driving aside the edge of Central Park. It stopped at the traffic light on the corner of 72nd Street. At that moment, Chapman knew who was inside that limousine. "I felt it," he told *People*. "My soul reached out to that car and I knew he was out there." The traffic light changed to green, and the limo turned left and stopped at the curb in front of the Dakota. "So I got up, and the car rolled up, and the door opened and Yoko got out. … Yoko was about 30 or 40 feet in front of him—weird. It was all meant to be. If they were together, I don't know if I could have shot him or not. But see, he was alone. … He looked right at me and I didn't say anything to him. And he walked by me. I know he remembered me because I had this hat … and I had my coat on, you know, I looked the same. I'm sure he [remembered me], but he didn't say anything."

Chapman no longer felt anger toward John. Rather, he felt nothing, not one emotion. His mind and his heart were quiet. "Dead cold quiet," he said.

And as John walked past, Chapman heard a voice in his head repeating, "Do it do it do it do it …"—a simple command that left no margin for misinterpretation.

"I turned, pulled the gun out of my pocket. … I don't remember aiming. I must have, but I don't remember drawing a bead. … I just pulled the trigger steady five times. … I remember thinking, The bullets are working."[25]

However randomly Chapman thought he was shooting, the rounds were well guided, four of them destined with unrelenting accuracy for John Lennon's torso.

---

25   *People*, March 2, 1987

Bang. Gone were the vocal chords that had passionately generated some of the most memorable performances in rock 'n' roll history—"Twist and Shout," "Day Tripper," "Help!"

Bang. Gone were the main arteries leading to the heart that had inspired words to some of the greatest love songs ever written—"In My Life," "I Want to Hold Your Hand."

Bang. Gone was the shoulder blade that had balanced and embraced his beloved Rickenbacker guitar.

Bang. Gone were all his beauty and talent, destroyed piece by piece, shot by shot.

Bang. As the last of the five bullets pursued its predestined path, gone was the legend, gone was the man who had founded and led the greatest rock 'n' roll band of all time.

John staggered up a few steps leading into an office, gasped, "I'm shot," and collapsed on the floor. His eyeglasses cracked but remained on his face. Blood poured from his chest and his mouth. The night man on duty rushed to help, removed his tie to use as a tourniquet, but couldn't decide where to put it because John's wounds were so scattered and severe.[26] The moment that had been 20 years in the making was swift and complete, nothing remaining in the end. This was John's final crescendo. Where were all of his gold record awards? Where were his earthly possessions? Where were his millions of adoring fans? Where was his God? Now, it was nearly over for John as he lay in his blood on the floor of the foyer of his Dakota apartment building.

Outside, on the sidewalk, breathing the distinctive fumes of gunfire, Chapman stood alone, deserted by his demons. "The devil dropped me flat," he said later. "I felt abandoned. I was hollow."[27]

For a moment, the scene was quiet. Then suddenly a loud, shrill scream emanated from within the building. Chapman's hands fell limp to his side, and Perdomo ran over with tears in his eyes and shook Chapman. The revolver fell to the pavement and Perdomo kicked it aside and began pleading

---

26   Goldman, p. 685
27   *Court TV*, Oct. 2, 2000

Fans display the New York Post's headline announcing Lennon's death.

with Chapman to leave. "But where would I go?" Chapman replied. He wasn't the same person as before he'd fired the gun. He returned his hand to his pocket and withdrew *The Catcher in the Rye*—the soft cover symbolically blood-red—and quietly began reading.

When the police arrived, they immediately realized John's condition was too serious to wait for an ambulance. "I turned him over," officer Anthony Palma said. "Red is all I saw." Palma and his partner lifted John on their shoulders—John's shattered bones cracking aloud—and carried him to a squad car, where they laid him in the back seat, then sped off toward the Roosevelt Hospital emergency entrance on Ninth Avenue. One of the officers asked, "Do you know who you are?" John nodded slightly, moaned, but did not speak.[28] His condition was critical. He lay still, his eyes closed. He was a spokesman for a generation, whose voice was struck silent.

Upon arrival at Roosevelt, John's heart had ceased beating. But realizing the magnitude of the circumstances, doctors desperately tried to revive him, going so far as breaking open his rib cage to manually massage his heart. But

---

28   *Newsweek*, Dec. 22, 1980

the Beatle was lost. "It wasn't possible to resuscitate him by any means," Dr. Stephan Lynn, the attending physician, told *Newsweek*. "He'd lost three to four quarts of blood from the gun wounds, about 80 percent of his blood." To *The New York Times*, he added: "The bullets were amazingly well-placed."

The devil and his demons always attend their victim's death, according to Arturo Graf, author of *The Story of the Devil*. Their presence assures a "one final and decisive temptation," he writes, an opportunity to create a distraction to prevent repentance. "They could catch in its flight, without a moment's delay, the sinful soul, now doomed through all eternity to be their companion; they could ... make the last agony more excruciating, more fearful. Surely, to die in a room full of devils, fierce and horrible, on a bed shaken by impatient, clawing hands [must be] a torture unspeakable." We can never know whether John was spared this final mortal terror. As he lay dying in the Dakota, he was well inside the periphery of gargoyles that may have prevented the demons from entering. But in the back of the police cruiser, in the gurney of the emergency room, such protection was absent.

As John's body grew cold at Roosevelt Hospital, the police carried Chapman into custody in another patrol car. He remained quiet until one officer commented to his partner, "I told you I felt it. I told you that something big was going to happen tonight. Remember what I said? This is history, man! This is history!"

In the back seat, Chapman smiled. He replied, "I am the catcher in the rye."[29]

---

29   Jones, p. 49

Here, There
And Everywhere:
Further Evidence

1) he hade to die it, the beetle, 2) he didhithim self.
— James Joyce

The last John Lennon album released un-posthumously, the one he signed for Mark David Chapman on December 8, 1980, was *Double Fantasy*. The first single released from that album was "(Just Like) Starting Over." The corresponding music video opens in a room containing some of John's most valuable possessions: Rickenbacker guitars and a Vox amplifier, amongst scattered pictures from his past. The camera scans the scene and momentarily stops on a shelf containing the James Joyce book *Finnegans Wake*.

It's obvious when viewing the video that John made a conscious decision to include the book. Ask any film director—prominent props don't happen by accident. Moreover, the book's title on the binding is by far the most conspicuous in the displayed collection. But why *Finnegans Wake*? John mentions in *The Beatles Anthology* that he read the novel. And as noted earlier, during the last year of his life he confided to Frederic Seaman that books he had been reading were causing him to reflect on his own death. Could *Finnegans Wake* be one of those books?

Who would even consider the idea that *Finnegans Wake* could possibly be a harbinger of the future? Well, in short, its author would. Biographer Richard Ellmann writes of Joyce: "He was forever trying to charm his life; his superstitions were attempts to impose sacramental importance upon naturalistic details. So too, his books were not to be taken as mere books, but as acts of prophecy. Joyce was capable of mocking his own claims of prophetic power—

he does so in one section of *Finnegans Wake*—but he still made the claims." Did these prophetic powers foretell John's death? And if so, could those prophecies have been encouraged by Satan?

First published in 1939, a year before John's birth, the book was as much an exploration for Joyce as for his readers. Asked what he was working on, the Irishman once responded, "I don't know. It is like a mountain that I tunnel into from every direction, but I don't know what I will find."[1] The title comes from a 19th

James Joyce, photographed in 1918, published *Finnegans Wake* in 1939. Did the book predict the assasination of Lennon?

century Irish drinking ballad about a hod carrier who falls from a ladder, bumps his head and is presumed dead. The beginning of the last line of the ballad—"thanam o'n dhoul, do ye think I'm dead?"—is an Irish phrase meaning "your soul from the devil."

As Joyce published sections of the work in the mid-1920s, the response was nearly unanimous: Huh? "Some [reviews] were tentative," Ellmann writes, "saying this presumably great book would require study; others were

---

1   Gose, p. 214

cavalier, dismissing it as madness; and others impudent, assuming it was an interminably protracted bad joke." His own brother, Stanislaus, called it "incomprehensible."[2] Writer Martin Amis remarked that it "reads like a 600-page crossword clue."[3] Joyce's wife, Nora, asked him, "Why don't you write sensible books that people can understand?"[4] And his friend and colleague Ezra Pound wrote, "Up to present I make nothing of it whatever. Nothing so far as I make out, nothing short of divine vision or a new cure for the clapp can possibly be worth all the circumambient peripherization."[5]

Joyce defended his book by explaining that it is set in sleep, which he could not accurately portray using ordinary prose: "One great part of every human existence is passed in a state which cannot be rendered sensible by the use of wideawake language, cutanddry grammar and goahead plot." He also declared, "The night world can't be represented in the language of day," and, "The night required and justified a special language."

Almost three quarters of a century has passed since its release but readers and literary critics still mostly agree that *Finnegans Wake* is at best pretentious, at worst nonsense, and either way a waste of reading time. The characters and plot are abstruse, and the syntax and vocabulary are so refabricated and punny that the whole text feels as if it were written it an esoteric dialect of a language slightly resembling English. In fact, to this day, no one really even knows what the book is about. But John liked it, and he even mimicked its meandering and scattered style in some of his own poetry and prose. More important to this discussion, though, is that many of *Finnegans'* passages bear an eerie resemblance to events that would transpire in John's life and death in the years and decades after its publication.

Several passages seem to relate directly to the cover of *Sgt. Pepper's Lonely Hearts Club Band*, which itself appeared to prophesize so much about John's fate. The hidden message in the drumhead, the funeral arrangements for a fallen musician, the name of the murderer, all emerge in a single passage. Joyce writes:

2   Ellmann, p. 625
3   Amis, p. 117
4   Ellmann, p. 590
5   Ellmann, p. 584

"The curt witty wotty dashes never quite just right at the trim trite truth letter; the sudden spluttered petulance of some **capItalIsied mIddle**; a word as cunningly hidden in its maze of confused drapery as a fieldmouse in a nest of coloured ribbons: ... and look at this prepromiminal **funeral**, engraved and retouched and edgewiped and puddenpadded, ... all those red raddled obeli cayenne**pepper**cast over the text calling unnecessary attention to errors, omissions, repetitions and misalignments. ... The ungainly **musicianlessness** so painted in sculpting selfsounder ah ha as **blackart**ful as a podatus and dumbfoiunder oh ho oaproariose as ten canons in skelterfugue: **the studioius omission of year number and era name from the date, the one and only time when our copyist seems at least to have grasped the beauty of restraint**; the lubricitous conjugation of the last with the first: the gipsy mating of a grand stylish **gravedigging** with secondbest buns (an interpolation: these munchables occur only in the Bootherbroiwth family of MSS., Bb – Cod IV, Pap II, Brek XI, LunIII, Dinn XVII, Sup XXX, Fullup **M D C** X C: the scholiast has hungrily misheard a **deadman**'s toller as a muffinbell." (emphasis added)

This passage suggests that there is yet another hidden message within the drumhead: "the studioius omission of year number and era name from the date." Further observation reveals, within "lonely hearts," a curious anagram: "slay hereon lt." L is the 12 letter of the alphabet, and T is the eighth letter after L: together they make 12/8, or December 8, the day John was killed.

The next page in *Finnegans Wake* contains more imagery that, when interpreted, foretells the events in front of the Dakota:

"Day the dicebox throws, whang, loyal six I lead, out wi'yer heart's bluid, blast ye, and there she's for you, sir, whang her, the fine ooman, rouge to her lobster locks, the rossy, whang, God and O'Mara has it with his ruddy old Villain Rufus, wait, whang, God and you're another he hasn't for there's my spoil five of spuds's trumps, whang, whack on his pigsking's Kisser for him."

American Heritage Dictionary defines "whang" as "a loud, reverberant noise," such as a gunshot from a revolver. In that passage, the word "whang" is used five times, equal to the number of bullets Chapman fired. The narrator seems to be the obdurate dealer of a rigged game of chance, one who has patiently waited an allotted time and is now savoring the moment of collecting the bet.

Whang. The first shot is fired. "Out your heart's bluid" signifies John's cardiac wound from a powerful blow ("blast ye").

Whang. The second shot is fired. "Oomen" is Chapman, who went by the nickname Nemo ("omen" spelled backward) as a YMCA counselor. Also, an "omen" is a prophetic sign that portends good or evil. "Rouge" and "rossy" (rosy) are words suggestive of the color red, the color of blood.

Whang. The third shot is fired. "Ruddy" is a British term signifying a reddish color—again, blood flowing from wounds.

Whang. The fourth shot is fired. The preceding "wait" suggests the demons are anticipating the violent outburst. Also, the word "trumps" is used. In card games, a trump is a suit that defeats all others. And the verb "trump" means to win or to get the better of an opponent, such as the devil getting the better of God in this game for John's soul.

Whang. The fifth and final shot is fired. "Whack on his pigsking's Kisser"— to strike with a sharp blow to the mouth or head. John is dead.

Shortly thereafter, the text appears to continue describing the *Sgt. Pepper* cover, specifically how a notable historic figure was dropped from the montage. In planning the cover shoot, each Beatle was asked to contribute ideas for famous and influential people to appear. John's list included Adolf Hitler, who was cut at the last minute.[6] The German leader's exclusion was so late

---

6   Womack, p. 137

that in photographs of the set, his cutout can be seen standing off to the side, where it had been literally relegated to the wings. From *Finnegan's Wake*:

> "Wanted for millinary servance to olderly's person by the Totty Askinses. Formelly confounded with amother. Maybe growing a moustache, did you say, with an adorable look of amuzement? … To all's much relief one's half hypothesis of that jabberfaw ape amod the showering jestnuts of Bruisanose was hotly dropped."

Hitler served in the military, and there were questions about his linage, his father having possibly come from Jewish descent.[7] He did, of course, grow a moustache that would certainly have been amusing if not for the fact that anything related to Hitler triggers reminders of his terrible legacy. And he would be "hotly dropped" from the cover of *Sgt. Pepper*.

Finnegans Wake also appears to reference the original *Yesterday and Today* "butcher" cover:

> "**Johns** is a different **butcher**'s. Next place you are **up town** pay him a visit. Or better still, come tobuy. You will enjoy cattlemen's spring **meat**. Johns is quite divorced from **baking**. Fattens, **kills, flays, hangs, draws, quarters** and **pieces**. Feel his lambs! Ex! Feel how **sheap**! Exex! His liver too is great value, a spatiality! Exe**ex**! **COMMUNICATED**." (emphasis added)

In addition to the grisly description of the cover photo, the passage also seems conspicuous in mentioning other details about John: In his last years, he lived in the Uptown neighborhood of Manhattan where, he told *Playboy* in 1980, he spent his time "baking bread and looking after the baby"; "sheap" is incorrectly spelled in exactly the same way as "Beatles"; and, if John truly sold his soul to the devil, then he was surely excommunicated from his religion.

Joyce also writes three times of a revolver:

---

7   Crowe, p. 80

"**One tall man**, humping a suspicious parcel, when **returning late** amid a dense particular on his home way from the second house of the Boore and Burgess Christy Menestrals by the old spot, Roy's Corner, had a barkiss **revolver** placed to his face with the words: **you're shot**, major: by an **unknowable assailant**."

"Afterpiece when the Royal **Revolver** of these real globoes lets regally fire of his mio colpo for the chrisman's pandemon to give over and the Harlequinade to begin properly SPQueaRking **Mark** Time's Finist Joke. ..."

"He got the charm of his optical life when he found himself (hic sunt **lennones**!) at pointblank range blinking down the barrel of an irregular **revolver** of the **bulldog** with a purpose pattern, handled by an unknown quarreler who, supposedly, had been told off to shade and shoot shy Shem should the shit show his shiny shnout out awhile to look facts in their face before being hosed and creased (uprip and **jack** him!)." (emphasis added)

The last two bits in the latter passage may relate to John's song "Hey Bulldog" from the *Yellow Submarine* album: "Jack knife, in your sweaty hands," he sings. "You think you know me but you haven't got a clue."

Another passage appears to discuss Yoko Ono (John's quiet muse), the tragedy of his life and the penalty he paid for his success:

"Sylvia Silence, the girl detective ... when supplied with informations as to the several facets of the case in her cozydozy bachelure's flat, quite overlooking John a'Dream's mews, leaned back in her really truly easy chair to query restfully through her vowelthreaded syllabelles: Have you evew thought, wepowtew, that sheew gweatness was his twadgedy? Nevewtheless accowding to my considewed attitudes fow this act he should pay the full penalty."

Even Chapman is mentioned in *Finnegans Wake*, right in the opening paragraphs where Joyce writes of the Oconee River in Georgia. The book begins in the middle of a sentence:

> "riverun, past Eve and Adam's, from swerve of shore to bend of bay, brings us by commodius vicus of recirculation back to Howth Castle and Environs.

> "Sir Tristram, violer d'amores, fr'over the short sea, had passencore rearrived from North Armorica on this side the scraggy isthmus of Europe Minor to wielderfight his penisolate war: nor had topsawyer's rocks by the stream Oconee exaggerated themselse to Laurens County's gorgios."

Stream Oconee, or the Oconee River, is in Laurens County, Ga. Why of all places would Joyce—who spent most of his life in Ireland and Switzerland—choose to write about the American state of Georgia? Chapman, of course, hailed from the southern state, and, interestingly, lived in an area prominent with Irish street names: Shamrock Drive, Dublin Drive, Kilarney Road, Shamrock Court, Irish Lane and Bellgreen Way. And Georgia is also the state where Mark obtained the five hollow-point bullets he used to kill John.

Joyce also writes:

> "He was one time our King of the Castle
> Now he's kicked about like a rotten old parsnip.
> And from Green street he'll be sent by order of His Worship
> To the penal jail of Mountjoy. Jail him and joy."

Chapman, king of the Little People who had lived in the walls of his Georgia home on Green Forest Drive, was later abandoned by his disapproving subjects when he chose to kill John. ("They were appalled," Chapman said later.

"They wanted nothing to do with this evil plan."[8]) He was later incarcerated at New York's Attica State Prison; incidentally, John included a song titled "Attica State" on his album *Sometime in New York City*.

In the third paragraph of the book, Joyce writes of "the great fall," a repeating theme in his story. As mentioned earlier, on the morning of December 8, when Chapman purchased a copy of *The Catcher in the Rye*, he randomly opened the book and read these words: "This fall I think you're riding for—it's a special kind of fall, a horrible kind." From *Finnegans Wake*:

> "The fall … of a once wallstrait oldparr is retaled early in bed and later on life down through all christian minstrelsy. The great fall of the offwall entailed at such short notice the pftjschute of Finnegan, erse solid man, that the humptyhillhead of humself prumptly sends an unquiring one well to the west in quest of his tumptytumtoes: and their upturnpikepointandplace is at the knock out in the park where oranges have been laid to rust upon the green since devlinsfirst loved livvy."

This passage mentions sending "an unquiring one well to the west." The phrase "gone west" is a euphemism for dying or death. Also, the sun sets in the west; on a compass, west has a bearing of 270 degrees (2 + 7 = 9). In Ancient Egypt the west was considered the portal to the underworld, or hell.[9]

In his song "I am the Walrus," John sings, "goo goo goo joob," widely thought to be adapted from *Finnegans Wake*'s "googoo goosth" phrase. The book additionally mentions "Livpoomark lloyrge hoggs one four tupps noying." And the following passage also seems clearly connected to The Beatles' and John's journey: "Its pith is full. The way is free. Their lot is cast. So, to john for a john, johnajeams, led it be!"

Jorn Barger, a Joyce critic and researcher who has written for the journal *James Joyce Quarterly*, summarizes the feelings of the literary world about the novel in question: "While none can deny that *Finnegans Wake* is *at the very*

8   Jones, p. 220
9   Ruiz, p. 97

least a locked box, current opinions vary widely on whether that box can ever be opened, and, if it were, what we might hope to find inside." In penning his last novel, Joyce's intentions were bold: At the outset, he said he wanted to write a history of the world.[10] Whether the final work is really about the world or history, or about himself, or about a dream—or is, as Barger suggests, "just a magnificently twisted gorgeous Celtic knot"—is open to a still-lively debate amongst those who study such matters. What is certain is that Joyce worked on *Finnegans Wake* for half his writing career, an astoundingly long time to create such a great literary mystery.

Was the devil in any way behind this creation? In the absence of hard evidence, who can be sure? We do know that some people in Joyce's life thought *him* at least a bit Satanic, including his brother, friends and a landlord. Moreover, Joyce also suspected as much. In the book *Joyce, Milton, and the Theory of Influence*, author Patrick Colm Hogan writes: "In 1936, Joyce said to his grandson, Stephen, a tale about the little town of Beaugency and the devil. In a postscript, Joyce identified himself with the feline-befriending Beelzebub. Much like the author of *Finnegans Wake*, 'The devil,' Joyce informed Stephen, 'mostly speaks a language of his own.' In addition, the name of this language sounds rather like a Wakean pun of babbling syllables on Beelzebub, 'Bellsybabble.'"

Finnegans Wake, Joyce's self-dubbed "dark night of the soul,"[11] appears to partly be a premonition of the life and the death of John Lennon. And if it was written at the subconscious urging of the devil, then the further connection between Satan and one of the greatest rock-'n'-roll legends of all time is solidified even more.

If we place the final minutes of John's life to music, creating a soundtrack from his own compositions, a few songs stand out as critical to include.

We can imagine Chapman waiting in the archway of the Dakota apartments. He has been there all day, and now it's nighttime, cold, dark and quiet. But he is determined. He knows John will be back, and murder is imminent. John's limousine is heading up Central Park West, and the song "Come Together" begins.

---

10   Ellmann, p. 537
11   Ellmann, p. 594

Shoot me. Shoot me. Shoot me. …
Here come old flattop, he come grooving up slowly.
He got juju eyeball, he one holy roller. …
One and one and one is three. …
Come together, right now, over me.
Shoot me. Shoot me.

The white limousine reaches 72nd Street and turns left. Mark stands up. The limo pulls to the curb in front of the Dakota, the door opens and Yoko gets out and walks past Mark. Then John emerges, making eye contact as he walks by. Mark fires five shots. "I am the Walrus" begins, the keyboard oscillating an ominous sound, like a police or ambulance siren.

Like pigs from a gun,
See how they run.
I'm crying. …
Stupid bloody Tuesday …
Mr. city policeman sitting pretty,
Little policemen in a row,
See how they fly. …
I'm crying. …
"Slave thou hast slain me. … Bury my body. … Oh untimely death!"

John manages to climb a few steps leading to a small office where he collapses. He bleeds from several wounds. Yoko screams. Police officers arrive to find John lying in a large pool of blood. They ask him, "Do you know who you are?" and he cannot speak. The song "Revolution 9" begins.

Number nine [turn me on dead man], number nine [turn me on
*   dead man] …*
Who can tell what he was saying? His voice was low and his eye
*   was high. …*

We'd better go to see a surgeon. ...
My broken chair, my wings are broken and so is my hair. ...
Must have hit between the shoulder blades. ...

As they race to Roosevelt Hospital, John dies, and his soul leaves his body. The song "#9 Dream" begins.

Two spirits dancing so strange ...
Dream, dream away.
Magic in the air, was magic in the air?

The police report lists the time of the shooting as 10:50 p.m. John was dead upon arriving at Roosevelt at 11:07 p.m., a time lapse of 17 minutes. The remaining minutes of John's life placed to music:

"I am the Walrus": 4 minutes, 34 seconds;
"Revolution 9": 8 minutes, 20 seconds;
"#9 Dream": 4 minutes, 48 seconds;
Total time: 17 minutes, 42 seconds.

It is only human to presume that Chapman committed this crime out of his own necessity. Happenings of this nature will always be perceived according to the strengths and weaknesses of our capacity to fully understand spiritual matters. But what if he was merely executing things preordained?

In the eight months between the murder and sentencing, Chapman was prodded and probed by countless psychologists, some deciding he was delusional, some concluding he was competent. But Jack Jones writes that despite the myriad opinions, many of the evaluators found Chapman's to be "among their most difficult cases to diagnose." They struggled, he explains, "to penetrate and describe the medical symptoms of a spiritual battle that Mark Chapman says has raged within him for his entire life."

Dr. Naomi Goldstein, the first psychiatrist to interview Chapman after the shooting, recommended to the court that he stand trial, admitting that she couldn't pinpoint what, if anything, was wrong with him. "Whatever Chapman's reasons for killing the rock superstar," Jones writes, "the psychiatrist came to the conclusion that those reasons were part of a complicated riddle that lay beyond the realm of modern psychiatry as she knew it."

But another of Chapman's inquisitors, a man of different discipline, uncovered the more-likely truth. Rev. Charles McGowan from Chapel Woods Presbyterian Church, where Chapman attended services while living in Georgia, phoned the murderer the day after his arrest and visited him the following week. After just one meeting, McGowan knew what had beset his old parishioner. The next day he told Chapman's wife, Gloria, "There is a dimension to this case that the secular psychiatric world would never understand. I believe there was a demonic power at work." Chapman eventually agreed, acknowledging that there were "spiritual matters" behind his actions.[12]

"I've been going through a torment for the last two or three months," he told McGowan. "It's a struggle between good and evil and right and wrong. … I just gave in."[13]

McGowan told *NBC Dateline* in 2005, "I think spiritual forces of darkness distorted his whole world view—almost whispering to him that this was God's ordained plan for him to take this evil out of the world. And I attribute that to the devil himself, quite frankly."

Again, Chapman concurred: "A small part of me," he said, "must be the devil."[14] Though Chapman claimed that the evil presence abandoned him outside the Dakota after he fired his revolver, he still battled the issue of possession once behind bars. In 1987, *People* magazine ran a three-part series on Chapman that discussed a breakdown in prison:

---

12   *People*, March 9, 1987
13   *People*, June 22, 1981
14   Jones, p. 66

"As the guards at Rikers Island reported it, [Chapman] destroyed a TV set, threw a radio and began taunting a fellow inmate in a high-pitched voice that warned of horrible tortures awaiting in hell. Guards quickly subdued Chapman and locked him in his cell, where he ripped off his clothes and began jumping around wildly, climbing the bars and 'screeching and hooting like a monkey.' He tore his Bible into small pieces and used them to stop up his toilet. As his cell flooded, he began throwing water at the guards and taunting them. When they opened his cell door he lunged at them, and it took six men to drag him into a van that took him to Bellevue [Hospital Center].

"There he did not answer to the name Mark Chapman, and he spoke to the doctors in voices they had not heard before—one a high-pitched, female voice, the other low, snarling and aggressively male. The voices identified themselves as Lila and Dobar, emissaries of Satan.

"It was Lila's first possession of a human ... and she was struck by the weakness of human vision and the human body. Dobar was the more powerful demon—thousands of years old, exceedingly well versed in Biblical scripture and a member of the Supreme Council in Hades, a ruling body whose power was only exceeded by Satan's. Chapman noted, however, that Lila had the power to release and contain Dobar; he thought perhaps this was because Satan didn't trust him. He said that both demons could read his mind and that their purpose in possessing him was to make a showing of Satan's presence in the world, using Lennon's murder as the vehicle."

Around that time, God also got involved in Chapman's incarceration. Chapman revealed as much in court on June 22, 1981, the day jury selection was to begin. Instead of letting the proceedings proceed, Chapman used the opportunity to withdraw his plea of "innocent by reason of insanity" and to instead plead guilty to the murder of John Lennon. He made the decision against the advice of his lawyer, Jonathan Marks. Acting Justice Dennis Edwards asked Chapman detailed questions about the sentencing process, including whether he understood the consequences of pleading guilty. Edwards offered to let Chapman change his plea again at a later date if a maximum sentence was to be handed down. Court transcripts show that Chapman declined:

Chapman: Your honor, I appreciate the court's offer ... that I would be allowed the option to return to the "not guilty" plea. I would like to tell you that I made the decision to plead guilty regardless of any such circumstances. So, if we did return to that position, I would still plead guilty.

[Edwards allows Assistant District Attorney Allen Sullivan, who would have prosecuted the case, to ask Chapman why he changed his plea.]

Chapman: It is my decision and God's decision.

Sullivan: When you say it is God's decision, and I ask this advisedly since certain representations have been made to me by Mr. Marks, did you hear any voices in your ears?

Chapman: Any audible voices?

Sullivan: Any audible voices?

Chapman: No, sir.

Sullivan: Before you made this decision did you indulge in any prayer?

Chapman: Yes, there were a number of prayers.

Sullivan: After you prayed did you come to the realization which you understand to come from God that you should plead guilty?

Chapman: Yes, that is His directive, command.

Sullivan: Is that a realization you came to within yourself inspired perhaps by God?

Chapman: No, I felt that it was God telling me to plead guilty and then probing with my own decision whether to do what

God wanted me to do, whether to do what I wanted to do, and I decided to follow God's directive.

Sullivan: So would you say at this time that this plea is a result of your own free will?

Chapman: Yes.

Edwards: All right. Have any threats been made to force you to plead guilty?

Chapman: No, your honor.

Edwards: Have any promises been made to compel you or induce you to plead guilty?

Chapman: Not in such words. But I have been assured by God that wherever I will go, He will take care of me.

Edwards: A good Christian ethic. I presume we all feel that God will assist us in times of need and emergency.

In exchange for the guilty plea, Edwards promised that the sentence would not exceed 20 years to life in prison. On August 24, that's exactly the punishment Chapman received. He was transported first to Ossining Correctional Facility, then to the maximum-security Attica Correctional Facility in upstate New York to serve out his sentence.

He didn't go alone. Chapman's demons accompanied him to Attica. McGowan had seen them. So had two chaplains at Rikers Island prison, and

Mark David Chapman as photographed from prison on March 6, 1998.

so had his wife, Gloria. "She believed the creatures from the dark side of his spirit were again taking possession of his mind," Jones writes. "She could see it in his eyes. She could hear them playing in the random, unguarded words that slipped from the corners of his conversation." Jones further reports that Chapman started burning red light bulbs in his cell, sang self-penned hymns to his demons, resumed praying to Satan and again became violent.

In 1985, Chapman finally retaliated against the evil within him. He conferred with yet another priest who agreed to pray simultaneously outside of prison at a prearranged time, and then Chapman began praying to God to exorcise his demons.[15] The prayer worked. Chapman told *People*: "[God] flooded me with peace. … Then—a complete surprise—He delivered me from about five or six demons. They came out. I ended up on the floor, groaning and making sounds and language very strange to me. …

"I was pacing in my cell, and my body was shaking, and all of a sudden I felt the Holy Spirit come down and say there were demons inside me. … And I asked in Jesus' name [for them to] come out. My face was snarling and it came out of my mouth, this *thing*, and it was gone. And I relaxed, and then I started breaking out in a sweat. Then there were more. I said, 'In Jesus' name, come out,' and the second one was worse. Then the third one came out, and *it* was worse. And I said, 'I'm ready, God, let's get them all out.'

"During that hour six came out. [They were] the most fierce and incredible things you ever saw or heard in your life—hissing, gurgling noises and different voices [coming] right out of my mouth.

"As they were leaving me, I felt essences of my personality departing from me that I'd picked up before. In other words, the way I was acting—cursing and things like this—weren't me, and when [the demons] came out I could sense these things coming out of my mouth, hissing and awful gurgling and grinding and I could feel that part of my personality was gone."

He further described the experience to Jones: "When [the demons] are coming out, there's a grinding inside you. When you really feel them is when they're coming out, with these squelched screams and cries and languages and cursings. You just feel this filthiness. It's like a shower when you're covered in filth, with filth in your nose, your hair, your ears. Filth caked to your skin."

It seems evident that a promise made to the devil by one man for worldly gain inexorably influenced the life of another. Possessed from birth and called

---

15   Jones, p. 226

into action by preternatural forces, Chapman's existence appears to have been dedicated to the fulfillment of a sinister will, leaving him virtually choiceless in the direction his life would take. With the power of the devil rooted in him since birth, Chapman tried to find peace and purpose, and he even tried to know God. But in the end it was to no avail. He was still made to execute the devil's deed. He still murdered John Lennon.

The filth was finally removed from Mark David Chapman's existence. His demons never returned. Though the devil left him, Chapman still resides in the dreary fortress of Attica. Five times he has been rejected for parole.

Shortly after 3 a.m. on December 30, 1999, 33-year-old Michael Abram of Liverpool stood outside George Harrison's 120-room mansion in Henley-on-Thames, England. A voice inside Abram's head said, quite clearly, "God is with you." Emboldened, he broke the glass of the double doors leading from the dark grounds into the kitchen. He stepped inside and lit a cigarette.

In an upstairs bedroom, George's wife Olivia lay awakened by the sound of the crashing glass. She roused her husband, who arose from bed and cautiously walked downstairs. His eyes met his intruder's, and George shouted, "Hare Krishna! Hare Krishna!" Abram misunderstood the Hindu mantra as a backward-spoken Satanic curse and ran at the former Beatle with a six-inch black-handled knife.[16]

"I tried to get into a room, but the key was stuck," George later told a prosecutor, "so I decided to tackle him by running towards him and knocking him over. We both fell to the floor. I was fending off blows with my hands. He was on top of me and stabbing down at my body."[17]

Abram's knife impaled George in the thigh, in the cheek, in his left arm. But the most notable pierces were two into his lung. "I vividly remember a deliberate thrust of the knife toward my chest and I felt my chest deflate and

---

16   *BBC News*, Nov. 15, 2000
17   Clayson, p. 451-2

the flow of blood toward my mouth," he stated in written testimony. "I believed I had been fatally stabbed."[18]

Olivia, hearing the scuffle, came from the bedroom and reached for the nearest household items she could use as weapons. She hit Abram first with a brass poker, then with a table lamp. George looked her in the eye. "I've never seen my husband look like that," Olivia said later. "I raised my hand and hit [Abram] on the back of the head as many times as I could, as hard as I could."[19] Then, with what help George could offer, she subdued their attacker until police arrived moments later.

Olivia suffered superficial injuries, while George was hospitalized with a collapsed lung. Doctors told the Associated Press that the knife narrowly missed severing his superior vena cava, a major vein that drains blood from the head and upper body. He was transferred to a hospital with a special chest-care unit, and was discharged on January 1. He made a full recovery from the wounds, but Olivia later asserted that healing from the trauma sapped George of the energy he needed to overcome the cancer that would succeed in killing him just two years later.[20]

What would cause yet another person to assault yet another Beatle? Investigators soon learned that Abram had committed the attack because, in his words, "The Beatles were witches, and George was the leader, a witch on a broomstick, who talked in the devil's tongue, an alien from hell."[21]

According to Alan Clayton, author of the biography *George Harrison*, Abram's friends and relatives said he lived in "a world inhabited by witches, devils and sorcerers" and had been exhibiting increasingly strange behavior leading up to the attempted murder. Abram believed he was hired by God to kill George Harrison. Clayton writes: "Mocked by children, who dubbed him 'Sheephead' because of his shocked, pale-yellow thatch, [Abram] would sit chain-smoking for hours—sometimes naked—on an upturned plant pot on his dismal balcony or roam the shopping precincts ululating Beatles numbers

---

18   The Associated Press, Nov. 16, 2000
19   Shapiro, p. 191
20   *BBC News*, July 5, 2002
21   Clayson, p. 450

to himself and lost in misery, paranoid self-obsession and lonely contemplation. Who were, he pondered, the four phantom menaces, spreading global consternation and plague?"

Abram's mother, Lynda, told the Associated Press that her son had been treated for problems stemming from a heroin addiction, and that he had become "obsessed" with and "possessed" by The Beatles. "He hates them and even believes they are witches," she said, adding that he had been running into pubs shouting about the band. "He started to wear a Walkman to play music to stop the voices in his head."

Abram had twice been admitted to mental hospitals, and twice had been released quickly due to altercations with staff. And in late 1999, just like Chapman 19 years before, he made two trips to his victim's town before committing his crime.[22]

The night of the attack, Abram was seen in a nearby pub. He appeared to be "real calm," said a local. "I saw him leave at about 6 p.m., and heard him say 'I've got things to do.'"[23] A few hours later, he breached George's 34-acre estate. According to the Associated Press, authorities couldn't determine how Abram slipped through security that included powerful lighting, closed-circuit cameras, electronic gates, infrared sensors, an alarm and ten-foot walls topped with razor wire.

22   Clayson, p. 450
23   *The Guardian*, Dec. 31, 1999

Final Judgment

Children, don't do what I have done.
— John Lennon, "Mother," 1971

Is it possible to prove beyond a reasonable doubt that John Lennon entered into a 20-year pact with the devil in exchange for riches and world fame? If a written contract was found, the proof would be extraordinary. But historically, few of these contracts have ever been discovered.[1] Perhaps they were burned or otherwise destroyed, or perhaps they were never even set with ink and paper, or perhaps they were kept by Satan. Short of that physical evidence, we can only rely on religious doctrine and occult knowledge, and on John's own words to Tony Sheridan at the height of The Beatles' popularity: "I've sold my soul to the devil."

But the facts in the case of John Lennon as a modern-day Dr. Faust are beyond coincidence: the dramatic rise of The Beatles; the unusual and mysterious response by fans described as spellbound and ecstatic; the hidden messages in Beatles material that foretold death; John's expressed remorse later in life; the cold fact that in 1980, John was aware that he would soon die; and finally his violent death at the hands of Mark David Chapman, an individual possessed by demons. Satan may not have given John any reason to mistrust. John desired instant fame and prosperity, not a heavenly virtue; and so plots

---

1 Anshen, p. 52

the devil. John was devoid of faith, possessed by doubt and lost to the spiritual world.

The relationship between Biblical warnings and occult practices and the consequences of such behavior are firm. The rise and fall of John and the prospect that he entered into an agreement with hell are uncanny—an apparent 20-year pact that began in 1960 ended with his violent death in 1980. John faithfully fulfilled the obligation of a devil's deal, to the letter, and the devil responded in kind. Fitting with Satan's obligation, John received his rewards quickly, giving him time to enjoy the remaining years of his life.

John left behind an admirable legacy. He offered the world hope and a push toward positive change, and he was inarguably one of the greatest musical visionaries and talents of the 20th century. He was human, though, and imperfect. His biggest mistake, unfortunately, was one that not only brought him unprecedented fame, but also haunted his adult life and doomed his earthly existence.

Many believe that nothing happens in this world without God's permission. And with the gift of free will, He grants us consent, at our own peril, to betray even Him. The evidence presented here suggests that John chose to do just that, chose to secure the favor of a maliciously benevolent being, chose to sell his soul to the devil. In this, John offended both humankind and God. And in the mortal end, God chose not to intervene on his behalf.

Many historical personages have been accused of entering into a devil's compact, and to these the name of John Lennon may be added. In the matter of the numerous death clues that were examined by a generation of fans, we all got it wrong. It wasn't Paul, after all. It was John.

Works Referenced

Books

Agrippa, Henry Cornelius. *Three Books of Occult Philosophy: A Complete Edition*. Llewellyn Worldwide. 1993.

Ambrosini, Maria Luisa and Willis, Mary. *The Secret Archives of the Vatican*. Barnes & Noble Publishing. 1996.

Amis, Martin. *Experience: A Memoir*. Hyperion. 2000.

Amorth, Gabriele. MacKenzie, Nicoletta V. (translator). *An Exorcist Tells His Story*. Ignatius Press. 1999.

Anshen, Ruth Nanda. *The Reality of the Devil: Evil in Man*. Harper & Row. 1972

Barrow, Tony and Newby, Julian. *John, Paul, George, Ringo And Me: The Real Beatles Story*. Thunder's Mouth Press. 2006.

Best, Pete and Doncaster, Patrick. *Beatle!: The Pete Best Story*. Plexus Publishing. 1985.

Brown, Peter and Gaines, Steven. *The Love You Make*. Penguin Putnam Inc. New York. New York. 2002.

Bugliosi, Vincent with Gentry, Curt. *Helter Skelter: The True Story of the Manson Murders*. W.W. Norton & Company. 1974.

Cavendish, Richard. *Man, Myth and Magic: The Illustrated Encyclopedia of Mythology, Religion and the Unknown*. Marshall Cavendish Corp. 1983.

Christie, Anne. *Simply Numerology*. Sterling Publishing Company. 2005.

Claiborne, Robert. *Loose Cannons & Red Herrings: A Book of Lost Metaphors*. W.W. Norton & Company. 1988.

Clayson, Alan. *George Harrison*. Sanctuary Publishing, Ltd. 2001.

Coleman, Ray. *Lennon: The Definitive Biography*. McGraw Hill Book Company. 1984.

Cross, Craig. *The Beatles: Day-by-Day, Song-by-Song, Record-by-Record*. iUniverse. 2005.

Crowe, David M. *The Holocaust: Roots, History, and Aftermath*. Westview Press. 2008.

Crowley, Aleister. *The Magical Diaries of Aleister Crowley: Tunisia 1923*. Weiser. 1966.

Davies, Hunter. *The Beatles*. W. W. Norton and Company. 1996.

Decoz, Hans and Monte, Tom. *Numerology*. Perigree. 2001.

Dowlding, William J. *Beatlesongs*. Simon and Schuster. 1989.

Drayer, Ruth A. *Numerology: The Power in Numbers*. Square One Publishers, Inc. 2003.

Du Noyer, Paul. *We All Shine On: The Stories Behind Every John Lennon Song: 1970-1980*. HarperCollins. 1997.

Ellmann, Richard. *James Joyce*. Oxford University Press. 1983.

Fix, Andrew Cooper. *Fallen Angels: Balthasar Bekker, Spirit Belief, and Confessionalism in the Seventeenth Century Dutch Republic*. Springer. 1999.

Goldman, Albert. *The Lives of John Lennon*. William Morrow and Company. 1998.

Gose, Elliott B. *The Transformation Process in Joyce's Ulysses*. University of Toronto Press. 1980. p. 214.

Graf, Arturo. *The Story of the Devil*. The Macmillan Company. 1931.

Harding, Elizabeth U. *Kali: The Black Goddess of Dakshineswar*. Motilal Banarsidass. 1998.

Hoffmann, Frank W. *Arts & Entertainment Fads*. William G. Bailey. Haworth Press. 1990.

Hogan, Patrick Colm. *Joyce, Milton, and the Theory of Influence*. University Press of Florida. 1995.

Jones, Jack. *Let Me Take You Down: Inside the Mind of Mark David Chapman, the Man Who killed John Lennon*. Villard Books. 1992.

Joyce, James. *Finnegans Wake*. Faber and Faber. 1939.

Koch, Kurt E. *Occult Bondage and Deliverance: Counseling the Occultly Oppressed*. Kregel Publications. 1972.

Lewisohn, Mark. *The Complete Beatles Chronicle*. Hamlyn, Octopus Publishing Group Limited. 2000.

Mathews, Shailer and Smith, Gerald Birney (editors). *A Dictionary of Religion and Ethics*. The MacMillan Company. New York. c 1921.

Matovina, Dan. *Without You: The Tragic Story of Badfinger*. Partners Pub Group Inc. 1998. p. 67.

Miles, Barry. *Paul McCartney: Many Years from Now*. Macmillan. 1998.

Millman, Dan. *The Life You Were Born to Live*. H.J. Kramer. 1995.

Norman, Philip. *Shout!: The Beatles in Their Generation*. Simon and Schuster. 2005.

Patterson, R. Gary. *The Walrus Was Paul: The Great Beatle Death Clues of 1969*. Dowling Press. 1996.

Reeve, Andru J. *Turn Me On, Dead Man: The Beatles and the "Paul-Is-Dead" Hoax*. AuthorHouse. 2004.

Reston, James. *Dogs of God*. Anchor Books. 2005.

Rosean, Lexa. *The Encyclopedia of Magickal Ingredients: A Wiccan Guide to Spellcasting*. Simon and Schuster. 2005.

Rosen, Robert. *Nowhere Man: The Final Days of John Lennon*. Quick American Archives. 2002.

Rudwin, Maximilian. *The Devil in Legend and Literature*. The Open Court Publishing Company. 1970.

Ruiz, Ana. *The Spirit of Ancient Egypt*. Algora Publishing. 2001.

Salinger, J.D. *The Catcher in the Rye*. Little, Brown and Company. 1951.

Seaman, Frederic. *The Last Days of John Lennon: A Personal Memoir*. Carol Publishing Group. 1999.

Shapiro, Marc. *Behind Sad Eyes: The Life of George Harrison*. Macmillan. 2002.

Shotton, Pete and Schaffner, Nicholas. *John Lennon In My Life*. Stein and Day. 1983.

Sibley, Ebenezer. *A Key to Physic, and the Occult Sciences*. Champante and Whitrow. 1798.

Spizer, Bruce. *The Beatles Are Coming: The Birth of Beatlemania in America*. 498 Productions. 2003.

Turner, Steve. *A Hard Day's Write: The Stories Behind Every Beatles Song*. HarperPerennial. 1994.

Turner, Steve. *The Gospel According to The Beatles*. Westminster John Knox Press. 2006.

Wenner, Jann and Reich, Charles. *Lennon Remembers*. Verso. 2001.

Westcott, W. Wynn. *Numbers: Their Occult Power and Mystic Virtues*. Health Research Book. 1996.

Womack, Kenneth and Davis, Todd F. *Reading the Beatles: Cultural Studies, Literary Criticism, and the Fab Four*. SUNY Press. 2006.

Yenne, Bill. *Gothic Gargoyles*. First Glance Books. 1998.

The Beatles Anthology. Chronicle Books. 2000.

The Encyclopædia Britannica: A Dictionary of Arts, Sciences, Literature and General Information. University Press. 1910.

Articles & Essays

Ashton, David. "The Vanished World of a Woolton Childhood with John Lennon."

BBC News. "Jury out in Beatle stab trial." Nov. 15, 2000.

BBC News. "Freed Beatle's attacker sorry." July 5, 2002.

Bucks County Courier. "Since Sen. Keller Asks Ban, 3 Local Girls Want Beatles." Aug. 9, 1966.

Catholic News Agency. "Famous exorcist: 'The devil loves to take over those who hold political office.' " June 6, 2008.

Chicago Sun-Times. "Chapman Odyssey Led to Murder." Zielenziger, Michael. Dec. 10 1980.

Daily Herald, The. "Lennon's Murderer Sentenced." Aug. 25, 1981.

Daily News Times, The. " 'Popularity' of The Beatles." Aug. 5, 1966.

Guardian, The. "How George Harrison became a target." Hopkins, Nick and Kelso, Paul. Dec. 31, 1999.

Independent, The (London). "Death themes in Lennon's last songs." Gray, Chris. Oct. 10, 2000.

Liverpool Echo. "Lennon's college pal spills the beans on Beatle's shoplifting sprees." Riley, Joe. Jan. 28, 2005.

London Evening Standard. "How Does a Beatle Live? John Lennon Lives Like This." Cleave, Maureen. March 4, 1966.

Los Angeles Times, The. "Beatles' Joke Backfires Million Times." Johnson, Pete. June 1966.

New York. "The Death and Life of John Lennon." Hamill, Pete. Dec. 20, 1980.

New York Times, The. "Son 'a different person,' suspect's father says." Clendinen, Dudley. Dec. 11, 1980.

New York Times, The. "A Return to Shea, Minus the Moptops," Barron, James. August 15, 2000.

New York Times, The. "Recalling the Night He Held John Lennon's Still Heart." Kilgannon, Corey. Dec. 8, 2005.

Newsweek. "Death of a Beatle." Dec. 22, 1980.

Oakland Tribune. "Beatle Boss Explains Christianity Remarks." Aug. 5, 1966.

Oakland Tribune. "Chicago Teen-Agers Still Adore Beatles." Aug. 13, 1966.

Peale, Dr. Norman Vincent. Syndicated editorial. Oct. 30, 1966.

People. "Descent into Madness." Gaines, James R. June 22, 1981.

People. "The Man Who Shot John Lennon." James R. Gaines. Feb. 23, 1987.

People. "In the Shadows, a Killer Waited." Gaines, James R. March 2, 1987

People. "The Killer Takes His Fall." James R. Gaines. March 9, 1987.

Playboy. Scheff, David. January 1981.

Rolling Stone. "Lennon Lives Forever." Gilmore, Mikal. Dec. 5, 2005.

Seattle Times, The. "Shocked by Teen-Age Beatle 'Orgy.' " Dr. Bernard Saibel. Aug. 1964.

Time. "The Messengers." Sept. 22, 1967.

Washington Post, The. "Squashed by The Beatles." Segal, David. Feb. 6, 2004.

Television

Court TV. "Mugshots." Oct. 2, 2000.

Frontline. "The Man Who Shot John Lennon." Nov. 28, 1995.

NBC Dateline. "The Man Who Shot John Lennon." Nov. 18, 2005

Index

Also From New Chapter Press

Boycott: Stolen Dreams of the 1980 Moscow Olympic Games—
By Tom and Jerry Caraccioli

With a thorough exploration of the political climate of the time and the Soviet Union's invasion of Afghanistan, this book describes the repercussions of Jimmy Carter's American boycott of the 1980 Olympic Games in Moscow. Despite missing the games they had trained relentlessly to compete in, many U.S. athletes went on to achieve remarkable successes in sports and overcame the bitter disappointment of a once-in-a-lifetime opportunity dashed by geopolitics.

*The Bud Collins History of Tennis—*By Bud Collins

Compiled by the most famous tennis journalist and historian in the world, this book is the ultimate compilation of historical tennis information, including year-by-year recaps of every tennis season, biographical sketches of every major tennis personality, as well as stats, records, and championship rolls for all the major events. The author's personal relationships with major tennis stars offer insights into the world of professional tennis found nowhere else.

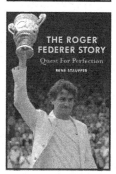

*The Roger Federer Story, Quest For Perfection—*By Rene Stauffer

Regarded by many as the greatest tennis player in the history of the sport, this authoritative biography is based on many exclusive interviews with Federer and his family as well as the author's experience covering the international tennis circuit for many years. Completely comprehensive, it provides an informed account of the Swiss tennis star from his early days as a temperamental player on the junior circuit, through his early professional career, to his winning major tennis tournaments, including the U.S. Open and Wimbledon. Readers will appreciate the anecdotes about his early years, revel in the insider's view of the professional tennis circuit, and be inspired by this champion's rise to the top of his game.

*On This Day In Tennis History—*By Randy Walker

Fun and fact-filled, this compilation offers anniversaries, summaries, and anecdotes of events from the world of tennis for every day in the calendar year. Presented in a day-by-day format, the entries into this mini-encyclopedia include major tournament victory dates, summaries of the greatest matches ever played, trivia, and statistics as well as little-known and quirky happenings. Easy-to-use and packed with fascinating details, this compendium is the perfect companion for tennis and general sports fans alike.

www.newchapterpressmedia.com